ACKNOWLEDGMENTS

This study began as a doctoral dissertation at Harvard University under the direction of Professor Heiko A. Oberman, who aroused my interest in the study of the late Middle Ages and Reformation. Now the study is so different from the dissertation that Professor Oberman should be associated with early virtues only, not with later vices.

Research trips were made possible by grants from the American Philosophical Society and the Bowdoin College Humanities Fund. The following libraries and archives were most helpful in providing materials and advice: Widener Library of Harvard University, the British Museum, the Bibliothèque Nationale, Friedsam Library of St. Bonaventure University, the St. Anna Kloster Library in Munich, the Bayerische Staatsbibliothek, the Bayerische Hauptstaatsarchiv, the Basel Staatsarchiv, the Frankfurt Stadtarchiv, the Stadtarchiv of Freiburg in Breisgau, the Nürnberg Staatsarchiv and the Strasbourg Archives et Bibliothèque de la Ville. The editors of the *Archive for Reformation History* and *Franciscan Studies* have generously permitted me to repeat certain arguments and information contained in articles published in those periodcials.

Profound appreciation is due to Mrs. Alice Yanok whose daily assistance and patient typing made possible my completion of this project while I served as dean at Bowdoin.

P. L. N.

ABBREVIATIONS

AF	*Analecta Franciscana* (10 vols.; Quaracchi, 1885–1926).	*FS*	*Franziskanische Studien* (Münster/W.-Werl, 1914–).
AFA	*Alemania Franciscana Antiqua* (Landshut-Ulm, 1956-).	MGHssm	*Monumenta Germania Historica: Staatschriften des späteren Mittelalters*, VI, edited by Heinrich Koller (Stuttgart, 1964).
AFH	*Archivum Franciscanum Historicum* (Quaracchi, 1908–).	SAB	Staatsarchiv Basel
Allen *Ep*	*Opus Epistolarum Des. Erasmi Roterdami*, edited by P. S. and H. M. Allen (12 vols.; Oxford, 1906–1958).	SAF	Stadtarchiv Frankfurt
		SAN	Staatsarchiv Nürnberg
AM	*Annales Minorum*, compiled by Luke Wadding (3rd ed.; Quaracchi, 1931–).	*WA*	*D. Martin Luthers Werke* (Weimar, 1883–).
BHM	Bayerische Hauptstaatsarchiv Munich	*WA Br.*	*D. Martin Luthers Werke, Briefwechsel* (Weimar, 1930–1948).

TRANSACTIONS

OF THE

AMERICAN PHILOSOPHICAL SOCIETY

HELD AT PHILADELPHIA
FOR PROMOTING USEFUL KNOWLEDGE

NEW SERIES—VOLUME 65, PART 8
1975

THE FRANCISCANS IN SOUTH GERMANY, 1400–1530: REFORM AND REVOLUTION

PAUL L. NYHUS
Associate Professor of History, Bowdoin College

THE AMERICAN PHILOSOPHICAL SOCIETY
INDEPENDENCE SQUARE
PHILADELPHIA

December, 1975

TO MY WIFE

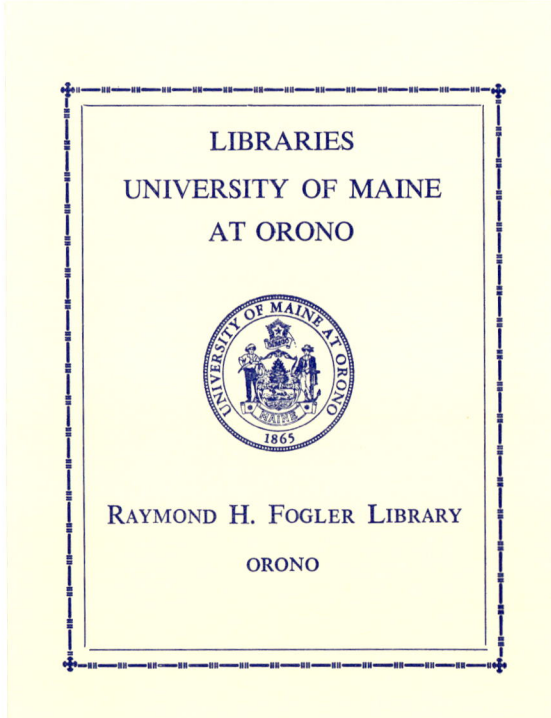

Copyright © 1976 by The American Philosophical Society

Library of Congress Catalog
Card Number 75-32621
International Standard Book Number 0-87169-658-4
US ISSN 0065-9746

THE FRANCISCANS IN SOUTH GERMANY, 1400–1530: REFORM AND REVOLUTION

PAUL L. NYHUS

CONTENTS

	PAGE
Introduction	5
I. The province in 1400	6
II. The friary as a city institution	8
III. The observant reform	10
IV. The intellectual habit	17
V. Years of confusion, 1517–1522	22
VI. Policies and theologies	25
VII. John Eberlin of Günzburg: reform and reaction	32
VIII. The beginnings of the Counter Reformation	36
Conclusion	42
Bibliography	44
Index	47

INTRODUCTION

The Franciscan Order receives considerably harsher treatment at the hands of Renaissance and Reformation historians than it does from medievalists. Most scholars speak in positive terms when discussing the early history of the order. They see St. Francis and his followers as heralds of a joyful message to the growing urban population of Europe.[1]

By the time of the Renaissance, however, the mendicant orders have become everyone's favorite whipping boy. When humanist writers wished to illustrate the perversion of pure Christianity, they cited mendicants. Erasmus pictured them as pompous but stupid, grasping while they begged. With the onset of the Reformation, the attack on the mendicants escalated from pillory and caricature to the closing down of their houses. Modern students of the period have echoed the judgments of the humanists and Reformers.[2]

What accounts for this revolution in judgment? Why are the heroes of the thirteenth century the villains of the sixteenth? One obvious answer to these questions would refer to the "life cycle" of religious orders. According to this interpretation, religious orders are at their best during their early years. As they become large, successful, and prosperous, their very prosperity corrupts them. They then are seen to enter a period of decay during which there is an horrendous gap between ideals and reality.[3]

To sustain such a thesis the proponents must amass evidence to show that corruption abounded among fifteenth-century friars. However, the evidence does not point in that direction at all. The fifteenth century witnessed a reform in the order which called it back to a closer observance of the original rules of poverty. Numerous reports referred to the Franciscan friaries as beloved and respected religious institutions in their host cities. The ravages of the decade 1520–1530 are astounding when contrasted with the favorable prospect for those friaries at the end of the fifteenth century. No simplistic description of "life cycles" of religious orders can account for the information at hand.

Historical research has focused on the charismatic years of the life of St. Francis and the tumultuous conflict initiated by the Spiritual Franciscans. Less attention has been paid to the friars in the late Middle Ages. Indeed, the final resolution of the Observant-Conventual conflict in 1517 provides a natural *terminus ad quem* for the early history of the order. Unfortunately such periodization—the neglect of the later Middle Ages and the separation between medieval and Reformation history—has made it difficult to provide a coherent account of the process by which the spiritual leaders of the thirteenth century became prime targets for criticism from the new spiritual leaders of the sixteenth century.[4]

This study seeks first of all to review the late Middle Ages. Reform had preoccupied the friars for the en-

---

[1] Favorable treatment of the first years of the Order is illustrated by Jeffrey Burton Russell, *A History of Medieval Christianity: Prophecy and Order* (New York, 1968), pp. 143, 144; Robert S. Lopez, *The Birth of Europe* (New York, 1967), pp. 385, 386 and Maurice Keen, *The Pelican History of Medieval Europe* (Aylesbury, 1971), pp. 156, 157. See also Friedrich Heer, *The Medieval World*, translated by Janet Sondheimer (New York, 1962), pp. 222–232 and Herbert B. Workman, *The Evolution of the Monastic Ideal* (London, 1913), pp. 271–316.

[2] Humanist critique of the friars is best illustrated by Erasmus's colloquy "Funus" in *Opera Omnia Desiderii Erasmi Roterdami* (Amsterdam, 1969-) I, 3: pp. 537–551. The Reformer's attack on religious orders is discussed by Bernhard Lohse, *Mönchtum und Reformation: Luther's Auseinandersetzung mit dem Mönchsideal des Mittelalters* (Göttingen, 1963). For an example of unremitting criticism of the friars, see G. G. Coulton, *Five Centuries of Religion* (4 v., Cambridge, 1923–1950), esp. 2–4. A balanced discussion of the state of the friars on the eve of the Reformation is provided by Lewis W. Spitz, *The Renaissance and Reformation Movements* (Chicago, 1971), pp. 315–317.

[3] Suggestions that success bred failure are made by John Moorman in *A History of the Franciscan Order From its Origins to the Year 1517* (Oxford, 1968), pp. 53–60; hereafter cited as Moorman and Russell, *op. cit.*, pp. 144, 145.

[4] The best recent survey of bibliography of Franciscan history is provided by Moorman, pp. 595–613. The neglect of the history of the friars in the late Middle Ages is illustrated by the paucity of works on the Observant reform. Both Moorman and Raphael M. Huber, *A Documented History of the Franciscan Order* (Milwaukee, 1944), hereafter cited as Huber, end their studies with the settlement of 1517. Holzapfel's study gives only passing mention to the impact of the Reformation. See Heribert Holzapfel, *Handbuch der Geschichte des Franziskanerordens* (Freiburg/Br., 1909), pp. 299, 300.

tire fifteenth century. Only after analyzing their internal conflict over reform, can one understand the shock they felt when external demands for reform in the early sixteenth century threatened the very existence of their order.

This study is quite deliberately written from the perspective of the friars. Most historical analysis of this period views events through the eyes of the friars' critics—the humanists and Reformers. This more common perspective is appropriate since the Reformers, in particular, were the successful protagonists of that time. However, a glance at the Reformation from the perspective of the friars serves as a useful minority report—not a portrayal of victors but a most illuminating description of the way the battle was fought.

I. THE PROVINCE IN 1400

Two centuries after the birth of the order, the Franciscans were well rooted in South Germany, so well rooted that their holdings and income were to become a source of considerable controversy. The South German Province consisted of some fifty houses reaching from Frankfurt, Strassburg, and Basel on the Rhine into Switzerland including Bern and Zurich and across Bavaria as far as Munich and Regensberg. The friars had established themselves within the walls of those cities destined to lead the German Renaissance. They had houses in Augsburg and Nuremberg, financial capitals of the great economic surge of the fifteenth century. In Heidelberg, Tübingen, and Basel, all destined to be important university cities, the Franciscans were present. As urban institutions, the friaries were in regular contact with the important economic and intellectual currents of the late Middle Ages.

A most conservative estimate would suggest that the fifty houses averaged twenty members each. This cautious estimate that the friars had attracted one thousand adherents in the province might well be increased by noting the size of several larger houses. In 1358 the Basel friary counted sixty adherents. The friary church in Strassburg had space for sixty in the choir. Quite possibly, the South German Province consisted of well over one thousand members.[1]

The Franciscan presence was marked physically by a friary in the city and in some cases friary churches as well. The reception of the Franciscans in the city was, in some cases, a governmental act by the city council granting them rights to the use of land or an existent structure.[2] Most of the residences dated from the first century of the order's activities in Germany. By 1400 the great friar churches had appeared in Basel, Strassburg, and Nuremberg. Such elaborate investment in real estate involved the friars in considerable fund-raising activity. Money was raised by the sale of indulgences and by the purchase of prayers and masses by the faithful. By 1400 the era of construction was completed. Their domiciles and churches helped shape the landscape of the cities.[3]

What contributions did the friars propose to make to the religious life of these cities? The founder of the order had envisioned a humble brotherhood of charismatic preachers unencumbered by the cares of this world. In the two centuries since the founding of the order, the friars had assimilated some characteristics of the secular clergy and other tendencies associated with traditional monastic orders.

First of all, the friars had fought diligently to obtain the right to perform certain clerical services. By 1400, they had clearly established authorization to preach, hear confession, and bury the dead. Frequent and bitter conflicts with the secular clergy regarding such privileges continued but the friars were able to prevail and offer clerical services.[4] Further, the friars began

---

[1] The best detailed study of the friaries of the South German Province is a typescript by Conrad Eubel, *Die Klöster der alten oberdeutschen Minoritenprovinz* intended by the author as a sequel to his *Geschichte der oberdeutschen (Strassburger) Minoriten-Provinz* (Würzburg, 1886), hereafter cited as Eubel, *Geschichte*. Although the typescript was never published, a copy is held by the Friedsam Library of St. Bonaventure University.

According to the Eubel typescript (pp. 8, 9) there were 57 active friaries in 1500, only 3 of which had been founded since 1308. The province was divided into 6 sub-units ("custodies") which oversaw the following houses:
1. Alsace
   Strassburg, Hagenau, Kolmar, Ruffach, Saarburg, Weissenburg, Schlettstadt, Offenburg
2. Rhine
   Mainz, Worms, Speyer, Heidelberg, Friedberg, Dieburg, Frankfurt/M., Gelnhausen, Oppenheim, Kaiserslautern, Breisach

3. Bodensee
   Lindau, Konstanz, Zurich, Luzern, Ueberlingen, Villingen, Schaffhausen, Burgdorf, Viktorsberg, Hausach
4. Schwabia
   Würzburg, Gmünd, Ulm, Hall, Esslingen
5. Bavaria
   Augsburg, Regensburg, Nordlingen, Bamberg, Nuremberg, Munich, Ingolstadt, Landshut
6. Basel
   Basel, Freiburg/Br., Bern, Freiburg/Sch., Mülhausen, Solothurn, Neuenburg/Rh., Thann, Königsfelden. See also Heribert Holzapfel, *Handbuch der Geschichte des Franziskanerordens* (Freiburg/Br., 1909), pp. 163, 164; Rudolf Wackernagel, "Geschichte des Barfüsserklosters zu Basel," in: *Festbuch zur Eröffnung des Historichen Museums* (Basel, 1894), p. 179; hereafter cited as Wackernagel, "Barfüsserkloster," and Dr. Rapp, "Strassburg," *AFA* 8 (1961): p. 10.

[2] Bernhard E. J. Stüdeli, *Minoritenniederlassungen und mittelalterliche Stadt* (Werl/W., 1969). A study of the establishment of Franciscan houses in French cities is provided by Jacques Le Goff, "Ordres mendiants et urbanisation dans la France médiévale, État de l'enquête," *Annales*, 25 (1970): pp. 924-946.

[3] G. Pickel, "Geschichte des Barfüsserklosters in Nürnberg," *Beiträge zur bayerischen Kirchengeschichte* 18 (1912): pp. 252, 253; hereafter cited as Pickel, "Nürnberg" and Wackernagel, "Barfüsserkloster," pp. 183, 184. See Ulrich Schmidt, *Das ehemalige Franziskaner-Kloster in Nürnberg* (Nuremberg, 1913).

[4] Eubel, *Geschichte*, pp. 17-28. See also Pickel, "Nürnberg," pp. 261-264 and W. Schaufelberger, "Zurich," *AFA* 15 (1970): pp. 78-83. For a list of papal and episcopal authorizations for South German Franciscans to preach and hear confession see

to hold offices within the hierarchy of the church. By the late thirteenth century a Franciscan, Nicholas IV, was elevated to the Papacy. At the same time, three bishops in South Germany were Franciscans.[5]

By 1400 the tradition of the brotherhood living together in common space had frequently given way to the introduction of private rooms in the friary. Although the common meal in the refectory remained as a symbol of the brotherhood, there were instances in the order as a whole in which leaders such as guardian and lector took their meals in separate accommodations. With thousands of adherents all over Europe, the order had been forced to limit the freedom of movement of its members. The guardian of each house was given control over the movement of the members of that house. Mandatory assignment from one house to another was frequently used by the hierarchy of the order to resolve disputes and to discipline recalcitrant friars.[6]

The education of novices was centered in one house in each of the six custodies of the South German Province. During the novitiate the friars were indoctrinated in the disciplined life of their rule, they were exercised in spiritual meditation and were taught to read the divine office.

The most capable friars were permitted to enhance their intellectual development through a pursuit of *studium generale*. Strassburg had been made the seat of such study in the South German Province early in the fourteenth century.[7] Such *studium generale* should not be confused with the offerings of the universities. These friary schools were intended to educate lectors for the various houses of the province. The lector, the most important figure in each house after the guardian, was to be a theologian in residence. His competence was to be such that he could give lectures to the friars on the Bible and the Sentences. This intellectual activity in the houses necessitated the collection of a friary library sufficient to support introductory theological instruction.[8]

The finances of each friary represented a curious compromise between the early ideals of the order and the present realities of size and establishment. The friars were required to continue begging but, in addition, they had certain regular sources of income. Payments in cash were made for prayers or masses to be said for the benefactors. In other cases, the friary committed itself to a perpetual reading of the holy office for a particular family in return for the gift of a house or other property. Rents were collected from such properties. In some cases, the friary found it necessary to enter litigation to collect their rents and protect their property rights.[9]

In the case of Basel, the friary records still available are particularly complete. They indicate that throughout the fourteenth century, there was extensive pious donation to the friary by the oldest families of the city. In particular, after the earthquake of 1356, there was a period of substantial giving, evidently to help the friary restore its residence and church. By the last decade of the fourteenth century, the golden era of new income for the house had come to an end. The incidence of new agreements for anniversary masses declined markedly at the beginning of the fifteenth century.[10]

Hence the friars presented a strange contradiction to the citizenry of the towns, a contradiction which was to emerge more and more clearly in the course of the fifteenth century. At one moment they might be begging on the street corner while at another moment they might appear before a city magistrate asking that a rental agreement for one of their properties be enforced. They were simultaneously mendicants and property owners.

In reality did the friars lead a life of prosperity or a life of poverty? There seems to be a general consensus that the friaries offered an adequate although not luxurious life. In some cases, there is evidence that friars continued to live in real need and poverty.[11]

The conflict between the Spirituals and the Conventuals ended in South Germany in the mid-fourteenth century. To be sure, four prominent Spirituals, William of Ockham among them, had taken up residence in Munich shortly after they fled in 1528 to the court of Lewis of Bavaria. However, after two decades Ockham and his protector were dead and with that the rebellion in South Germany ended even though some Spirituals continued to pursue their cause in France and Italy. When the Observant movement came to the South German province its proponents specifically disassociated themselves from the heritage of the Spirituals.[12]

Such was the position of the friars in 1400—established in the cities, owning property, preaching, and ministering to the people, but not yet fellow citizens; part of the landscape of the city but still separated out for a special spiritual calling. The tensions of this position were to trouble the friars for another century

---

Max Straganz, "Zur Geschichte der Minderbrüder im Gebiete des Oberrheins," *Zeitschrift des kirchengeschichtlichen Vereins für Geschichte, christliche Kunst, Altertums-und Litteraturkunde des Erzbistums Freiburg*, N.F., 1 (1900): pp. 328, 329. Many papal and episcopal privileges to preach and hear confession are found in that portion of the provincial archives preserved in the Lucerne Staatsarchiv. See for example SAL 519/9231, 519/9233, 519/9234, etc.

[5] Wackernagel, "Barfüsserkloster," pp. 169, 170.
[6] Moorman, pp. 361, 362.
[7] Rapp, *op. cit.*, pp. 12, 13.
[8] Moorman, pp. 366, 367.

[9] A general description of the order's adherence to the rule of poverty in the fourteenth century is found in Moorman, pp. 353–360. A specific discussion of the Strassburg friary is provided by Rapp, *op. cit.*, pp. 19–22. For further literature see below, chs. II. and III.
[10] Wackernagel, "Barfüsserkloster," pp. 177–184.
[11] Moorman, p. 358; Rapp, *op. cit.*, p. 22.
[12] Moorman, pp. 320–336. *Cf.* Parthenius Minges, *Geschichte der Franziskaner in Bayern* (Munich, 1896), pp. 22–24. Regarding the Observants' rejection of the heritage of the Spirituals see below pp. 14, 15.

and contribute to the destruction of many of the houses in the great upheaval of the early sixteenth century.

II. THE FRIARY AS A CITY INSTITUTION

The friars' attempt to protect their integrity and independence has been seen primarily as a struggle to hold to the ideals of poverty. Freedom from financial entanglements has been equated by historians with freedom to pursue spiritual goals.

A quite different challenge to the independence of the order has not received sufficient attention. In the course of three centuries, the friaries became increasingly "secularized" in their host cities. To be sure, financial support linked them to a wealthy constituency. However, the kinds of services they were asked to render, the activities in which they were permitted to engage, were defined by the political and social forces of the city. Benevolent in intention, unplanned in its growth, and seldom resisted by the friars, this control gradually tied the friary to the cultural spirit and political decisions of the cities.

THE FRIARIES AND CITY COUNCILS

The most obvious assertion of power over the friaries was made by the city councils. The councils which had permitted the houses to be established on land inside their walls found it necessary from time to time to specify the legal and financial position of the friaries in their midst.

The city governments themselves found their authority expanded and threatened in turn by a constantly shifting power matrix involving bishops, local princes, and the emperor. In a time of transition from episcopal to imperial control, the city governments sought opportunities to enhance their own autonomy. By the end of the fifteenth century, Basel, Strassburg, Augsburg, Nuremberg, Worms, Speyer, and Regensberg all were imperial cities hosting Franciscan houses.

Below the rank of imperial cities were those less distinguished towns subject to jurisdictional claims by local princes. Whatever the rank of the city, the changing fortunes of war and finance could enhance or diminish the prerogatives of the city council. Mainz, for instance, lost its status as an imperial city in 1462.[1]

Although the power of the merchant oligarchies in these cities was subject to the winds of change, one theme was constant throughout the fourteenth and fifteenth centuries. In those cities which grew in prosperity and power, there was a corresponding growth in the competence of the city council in ecclesiastical affairs. Gradually the lands and building of the church, the person of the clergy and their activities in the city were more closely regulated by the council. More often in a spirit of benevolent supervision than adversary conflict, the councils assisted, supervised, and regulated the work of the friars. The implications of that control were not clear until the Reformation erupted.

FRANKFURT, NUREMBERG, AND BASEL

The attainment of control over ecclesiastical affairs by the Frankfurt City Council was the result of deliberate council policy. By the last decade of the fourteenth century, it was clear that the Council was determined to have jurisdiction over all clergy equivalent to that exercised over lay citizens. Further, the Council was determined to stop the shrinkage of the tax base which was being caused by the increase in land holdings of ecclesiastical institutions. Religious houses in particular were contributing to this problem by acquiring more and more properties in return for a promise to hold perpetual masses for the living and deceased members of the donor family.

The special legal status of the clergy when combined with their position as landowner, created another aggravation for lay citizens. The clergy would refer legal questions regarding disputed land ownership to the Episcopal Court in Mainz. Further, some of the religious orders had begun to compete directly with local merchants. For example, a religious house which had long manufactured wine for its own use might begin to sell excess production. Local wine merchants complained, understandably enough, that such tax-free competition was unfair. The City Council was concerned not only to keep economic competition on an equal basis, but in addition, to seize an opportunity for a new source of tax revenue.

The conflict in Frankfurt took many strange turns. At one time the mendicant orders who had suffered less from City Council initiatives sided with the Council in its attempts to extend its jurisdiction over the secular clergy. In 1407 the Council bought the consent of the archbishop of Mainz to its extension of jurisdiction by sending him 4,600 gulden. Regardless of the alliances of the moment, the Council made steady progress in reaching its goals. A series of "compromises" was arranged in the first decades of the fifteenth century which established the power of the Council in regard to taxation and legal jurisdiction.[2]

The collaboration between the City Council and the mendicants did not preserve the latter from the inroads of Council jurisdiction. In 1481 the mendicant orders agreed to a settlement with the Council. The terms of the settlement called for city taxation of properties held by the mendicants in the town and income earned by those orders in the town.[3]

In the case of Nuremberg, City Council control of religious affairs took the form of well-intentioned assistance. By the mid-fifteenth century the Council had established its role as protector and defender of the Church. A supervisor of ecclesiastical affairs (*Kirchenpfleger*) was appointed by the Council to oversee matters of property and finance.

---

[1] Hans Planitz, *Die Deutsche Stadt im Mittelalter* (2nd ed., Graz-Cologne, 1965), pp. 168–183.

[2] Herbert Natale, *Das Verhältnis des Klerus zur Stadtgemeinde im spätmittelalterlichen Frankfurt* (Frankfurt, 1957), pp. 15–55.

[3] *Ibid.*, pp. 44–49.

These actions were based in part on the Council's claim to total control of land use within the city. Further, numerous citizens had made pious endowments to religious houses in return for the perpetual reading of anniversary masses. These agreements were attested to by city officials and the execution of the agreement was a matter for governmental supervision.[4]

The sale of indulgences in Nuremberg was often resisted by the Council during the second half of the fifteenth century. Numerous indulgence bulls were issued to gather funds for crusades against the Turks and the Hussites. The Franciscans were frequently chosen as purveyors of these indulgences, especially during the reign of Sixtus IV (1471–1484), the Franciscan pope. But as the crusades floundered or failed to materialize at all, the papal agents were greeted with official hostility.

The Nuremberg citizenry had joined more than one thousand strong in a Turkish crusade in 1456 which ended as a miserable failure. Thereafter their reactions were more skeptical. The Council opposed the sale of indulgences within the city not only because they were skeptical of the uses to which the money would be put, but also because they did not want money drained out of the city.[5]

An incident involving Franciscan sales of a Hussite crusade indulgence in 1468 is illustrative of the public reaction. A Franciscan agent of the bishop of Breslau had completed his work in Nuremberg when the Council called him back to answer charges regarding his activities. In a deposition the agent denied a whole series of scandalous charges circulating in the city. He had been accused of gathering inordinate sums of money from the town folk. Rumor had it that he had sent twenty-five hundred to three thousand gulden ahead of himself out of the city, that he had diverted some of the money for his own luxury and that he had climaxed his performance by slipping out of town at night. The agent vehemently denied the charges but admitted that he had sent four hundred and twenty-eight gulden out of the city while keeping eleven gulden for his own use.[6]

The opposition to papal money-raising efforts in Nuremberg was clearly pragmatic, not ideological. Thus Sixtus IV was able to overcome the Council's resistance to the Turkish tax by assigning one-third of the total income to local hospitals.[7]

Basel was another city which exemplified the gradual extension of Council authority over ecclesiastical affairs previously controlled by the bishop. The attainment of citizenship by various elements of the clergy subjected them to Council jurisdiction.[8] Friary finance also became a matter of governmental concern. Contracts for anniversary masses were supervised by municipal officials such as the *Vogt,* formerly an imperial representative but by the late fifteenth century subject to control by the Council.[9]

The Franciscans in Basel were caught in the middle of a spectacular conflict between the Council and the papacy in 1482. A Dominican, Andreas Zamometic, archibishop of Granea, declared the convocation of a general council in Basel to reform papal errors, chief of which was the Turkish crusade bull. This bizarre declaration announced to the town's people in the cathedral immediately evoked the wrath of a papacy, which had only recently survived a general council in Basel.

The City Council by contrast had happy memories of the fame and profit which the General Council had brought. Hence, the papal demands for the arrest of Andreas were resisted. These disagreements quickly escalated into a major storm. The papacy first declared an interdict against the city and then called on the rulers of Europe to "crusade" against Basel.

In spite of the interdict, Basel's resistance continued. Church doors displayed the City Council's defense of its resistance next to the declaration of interdict. All the clergy save the Franciscans disobeyed the papal decree and continued to offer ecclesiastical services. Only the Franciscan church was closed. The friars refused to abandon a pope who was one of their own and under attack because he had authorized their order to sell indulgences. In the end papal pressure resulted in the imprisonment of Andreas who took his own life. The incident dramatized the close tie of most of the clergy

---

[4] Gerald Strauss, *Nuremberg in the 16th Century* (New York, 1966), pp. 155, 156; hereafter cited as Strauss, *Nuremberg* and Emil Reicke, *Geschichte der Reichstadt Nürnberg* (Nuremberg, 1896), pp. 689, 690. For a more general discussion of this topic in late medieval Germany see Alfred Schultze, *Stadtgemeinde und Reformation,* in: Recht und Staat in Geschichte und Gegenwart 11 (Tübingen, 1918): pp. 12–17. For an example of Nuremberg City Council responsibility to enforce an anniversary mass contract see SAN, D Urk., No. 168.

In Augsburg also the city fathers oversaw many aspects of friary affairs. The role of the *Klosterpfleger* in Augsburg is described by Rolf Kiessling in his *Bürgerliche Gesellschaft und Kirche in Augsburg im Spätmittelalter,* in: Abhandlungen zur Geschichte der Stadt Augsburg 19 (Augsburg, 1971): pp. 145–150.

[5] Reicke, *op cit.,* pp. 437, 438, 690–692. *Cf.* Irmgard Höss, "Das religiöse Leben vor der Reformation," in: *Nürnberg— Geschichte einer europäischen Stadt,* edited by Gerhard Pfeiffer (Munich, 1971), p. 140.

[6] SAN, Franziskaner Kl. Nbg., No. 4. *Cf.* Pickel, Nürnberg," *Beiträge zur bayerischen Kirchengeschichte* 19 (1913): pp. 19, 20.

[7] Fortunatus Hueber, *Dreyfache Cronikh von denen Orden-Ständen des h. Vatters Francisci* (Munich, 1686) 3: col. 396; hereafter cited as Hueber. *Cf.* Amalie Stahl, "Nürnberg vor der Reformation" (unpublished Ph.D. dissertation, Erlangen University, 1949), pp. 64–68.

[8] Rudolf Wackernagel, *Geschichte der Stadt Basel* (3 v., Basel, 1907–1924) 2, 2: pp. 735, 736; hereafter cited as Wackernagel, *Geschichte.*

[9] For examples of municipal supervision of anniversary masses and other real estate affairs of the Basel friary see SAB, Barfüsser Urkunden; No. 119, 1400; No. 127, 1402; No. 129, 1404; No. 136, 1408. A discussion of the office of *Vogt* is provided by Wackernagel, *Geschichte* 1: pp. 44–49, 73, 74; 2, 1: p. 333.

THE SUPPORTING CONSTITUENCY

Financial support from the wealthy and powerful both enriched and troubled the friaries during the fifteenth century. The plentiful records available in Nuremberg indicate the close ties between the friary and the patrician families. After the Nuremberg friary was reformed by the Observants in 1447, an inventory was drawn up of the altarware and clerical robes which were considered too extravagant to remain in use. The inventory indicates that many of these items removed from the friary were inscribed with family insignia. Of the approximately eighty-five insignia reported in the register, half are those of patrician families. Eighteen patrician family names were represented, some repeatedly. The families whose names were inscribed most frequently were the Pfinzing family whose name was recorded six times and the Pirckheimer family whose name was found on four separate items.[11] The mass calendar in which was recorded the anniversary masses to which the friary was obligated displays a similar pattern. Many of the patrician families had arranged to have such spiritual services rendered by the Franciscans.[12]

Similar patterns can be observed at Strassburg and Basel. During the first half of the fifteenth century, the patriciate and nobility were frequent donors to the Strassburg friary. However, after 1415, the Strassburg friary experienced a general decline in the number of friars in residence and financial support from the powerful and wealthy classes. At Basel, the records of the fourteenth and fifteenth century burials in the friary include the names of nobility as well as prominent merchants.[13]

Although the leading families supported the friaries and sought the spiritual benefits available there, there is less evidence that they actually joined as members. A study of Nuremberg's religious houses suggests that although the patriciate was generous with funds, it contributed few sons.[14] There were exceptions. Conrad von Bondorff, provincial of the order at the turn of the century, was of noble birth.[15] The father of Willibald Pirckheimer entered the Nuremberg friary in his last years to die there in 1501.[16] But in spite of these exceptions the wealthy and powerful were more frequently benefactors than members.

Local princes also had a powerful hand in the affairs of the houses in Heidelberg and Munich. The Observant Reform was introduced into the South German province from Heidelberg where the prince of the Rhine Palatinate instituted the reform at his wife's insistence.[17] Prince Frederick was buried in the Heidelberg friary in 1476.[18]

The Munich friary was closely tied to the court of the Bavarian rulers. In the fourteenth century the Munich friary hosted the anti-papal propagandists who supported the cause of Lewis of Bavaria. During the fifteenth century, the princes purchased anniversary masses from the Munich friars and then late in the century supported the introduction of the Observant Reform into Bavaria.[19]

CONCLUSION

The friars set out to minister to the city while obeying a Rule forbidding worldly entanglements. These two goals were often in conflict. The very protection and nurture of the friars' ministry by municipal authorities grafted the houses into the political and social body politic of the city. This subtle "secularization" of the friaries was little debated in its own time. Discussion of observance of the order's rule which focused on individual friars simply neglected the institutional question. Although strict rules had been established to limit the intercourse of each friar with the world, few limits were set on the "worldliness" of the friary as a corporate entity.

III. THE OBSERVANT REFORM

The Observant struggle for power against the Conventuals convulsed the order throughout the fifteenth century. The triumph of the Observants in 1517 necessitated a total reshaping of the Franciscan hierarchy. From the first appearance of Observants in Heidelberg in 1426, the South German Province was torn by controversy. By the final quarter of the century, the Observants had captured the most influential houses in the province. The power they had attained was recognized officially in the settlement of 1517 which instituted two separate ruling hierarchies for the contending parties.

---

[10] Wackernagel, *Geschichte* 2, 2: pp. 875–885, and Nicholas Glassberger, *Chronica,* in: Analecta Franciscana 2 (Quaracchi, 1887): pp. 482–484; hereafter cited as Glassberger. See also Hueber, 3: cols. 391–396.

[11] SAN, 7 farb, Alph., No. 2029.

[12] Stahl, *op. cit.,* pp. 152, 153.

[13] Rapp, *op. cit.,* pp. 18–24 and Wackernagel, "Barfüsserkloster," pp. 239–243. Kiessling's study demonstrates that in Augsburg the great surge of financial support for the Franciscans began about 1380 and lasted until the mid-fifteenth century. Donations were given by a wide variety of classes encompassing hand workers as well as members of the patriciate. See Kiessling, *op. cit.,* pp. 263, 264.

[14] Stahl, *op. cit.,* pp. 153, 154.

[15] Florentinus Landmann, "Zum Predigtwesen der Strassburger Franziskanerprovinz in der letzten Zeit des Mittelalters," *FS* 15 (1928): p. 108.

[16] *Willibald Pirckheimers Briefwechsel,* edited by Emil Reicke (2 v., Munich, 1940–1956) 1: p. 7.

[17] See below pp. 12, 13.

[18] Hueber, 3: col. 376.

[19] BHM; K U München Franziskaner, II/2; K U Amberg Franziskaner, 5; K U Landshut Franziskaner III/2. Cf. Dagobert Stöckerl, "Das alte Franziskanerkloster in München in seinen Beziehungen zum bayrischen Fürstenhaus bis zum Reformjahr 1480," in: *Festgabe Alois Knöpfler* (Freiburg/Br., 1917), pp. 353, 354. See also Romuald Bauerreiss, *Kirchengeschichte Bayerns* (6 v., Erzabtei St. Ottilian, 1950–1965) 5: pp. 68–75.

THE NECESSITY OF REFORM

The state of the Order about 1400 was the subject of intense debate between Observants and Conventuals. Any contemporary attempt to reappraise that situation must first sift through the varying standards which have been used to judge the order.

First, there were the absolute standards of poverty and humility laid down by St. Francis. When St. Francis approached Pope Innocent to request official sanction for his order, the pope is reported to have commented that St. Francis had set an impossible standard. He inquired as to what would happen in succeeding years as the impossibility of these goals became manifest. Eventually, he was persuaded to sanction the order with the hope that divine assistance would allow mere mortals to meet the standards outlined by St. Francis.[1]

Innocent's inquiry contained a note of prophetic wisdom. As St. Francis's movement outgrew the limits of a small charismatic brotherhood and became a European-wide institution with thousands of members, the ideals of the founder became increasingly unrealistic. Even the Observants compromised the absolute standards of the founder. The question was not if such a compromise should be made but how much compromise should be allowed.

Much of the source material available for the fifteenth century has been compiled by partisans in the Observant-Conventual dispute. Nicholas Glassberger, whose chronicle is a prime source for the South German Province in the fourteenth and fifteenth centuries, completed his work in the Observant house in Nuremberg in 1508. Glassberger portrayed the spread of the Observants as one triumph after another. On the other hand, the chronicles prepared by Tschamser and Müller in the early eighteenth century sought to vindicate the Conventuals by emphasizing the grasping tactics used by the Observants to seize houses.[2] From these partisan sources one derives diametrically opposed views regarding the need for reform and the achievements of the Observant movement.

A reassessment of the need for reform can best proceed by reviewing an evaluation made outside the order. The *Reformatio Sigismundi*, a call for sweeping reform of secular and religious institutions, was widely accepted in the fifteenth century as a statement of the agenda for the time. The first version of this document was probably prepared in Basel and reflected the reforming spirit of the conciliar period.[3]

The *Reformatio* urged that religious orders be forbidden to bury the dead in their houses because they had used this privilege to service the powerful and the wealthy in return for gain. Further, it proposed that private anniversary masses dedicated to wealthy benefactors should be abolished. In their place one common mass was to be said weekly for all who had died in the parish. Instead of collecting money through endowments and anniversary masses, the mendicants should return to begging as their founders had intended. Then, society would not be faced with a spectacle of mendicant houses purchasing organs or friars aggressively pursuing an education in order to enter lucrative professions such as law and medicine. In sum, the mendicants should more strictly observe their own rules.[4]

This call for reform centered on financial matters. Violations of celibacy which became so controversial in the early Reformation did not figure prominently in the reform literature of the fifteenth century.[5] Assuming that observance of poverty was the sticking point, how affluent was life in the unreformed friaries? Extant information provides only a partial answer. In several cities—Basel, for example—an extensive record of endowments to the Franciscan house is retained in the city archive. However, our information is not complete enough to compare income with expenses and reach conclusions regarding the relative poverty or opulence of life in the friaries in the early fifteenth century. Cajetan Schmitz made the most extensive study of this question. He noted that, although we do have statistics regarding the income available from anniversary masses in several cities, we do not know the expenses encountered in celebrating those masses. Candles had to be purchased and the celebrant and preacher paid. Further, our information regarding the number of friars resident in a given house is incomplete so that an accurate balance sheet cannot be drawn up.[6]

Some anecdotal reports are available. The friars of Strassburg reported to the City Council that the cessation of anniversary masses in 1524 meant a loss of 150 pounds of annual income to their friary. This figure may, of course, have been an overstatement in order to impress the Council with their impoverished state.[7] As was noted earlier the incidence of new gifts diminished in Basel after 1400.[8] Taken together, the information suggests that no friary was completely self-sufficient because of its endowments.

Hence the friars had to go into the streets and beg in order to meet the needs of the friary. The resulting

---

[1] Moorman, pp. 18, 19. For a review of recent literature on the development of mendicant movements, see André Vauchez, "La pauvreté volontaire au Moyen Age," *Annales* **25** (1970): pp. 1566–1573.

[2] See below p. 14. For examples of more modern authors defending the Conventuals see Eubel, *Geschichte,* pp. 62–67, and for the Observants see Minges, *op. cit.,* pp. 41–65.

[3] Introduction to *Reformation Kaiser Sigismunds,* MGH, ssm VI (1964), pp. 4–10, by Heinrich Koller, editor.

[4] *Ibid.*, pp. 160–162, 190, 204, 205, 222.

[5] For an isolated example of complaints that a guardian of the Nuremberg friary consorted with women see below p. 13. *Cf.* Cajetan Schmitz, *Der Zustand der süddeutschen Franziskaner-Konventualen am Ausgang des Mittelalters* (Düsseldorf 1915), pp. 8–56.

[6] *Ibid.*, pp. 71–88. A thorough analysis of friary holdings in Zurich arrives at approximately the same conclusion. See Schaufelberger, *op. cit.,* pp. 83–114.

[7] Rapp, *op. cit.*, pp. 19, 20.

[8] See above p. 7.

combination was, in certain respects, the worst of all possible worlds. Although the mendicants were known to receive substantial endowments from wealthy families, they appeared in the streets calling out that they needed alms if they were to survive. It was just this contradiction which was seized upon by the enemies of the friary. Critics of the friars such as Felix Hemmerlin of Zurich and Sigmund Meisterlin of Nuremberg pointed to the gap between the ideal and reality in financial matters. Further, the Hussite movement which extended its influence into Germany emphasized that the clergy should live in humble circumstances.[9] The dilemma envisioned by Pope Innocent was indeed the cause of abiding dissatisfaction for the friars.

THE ORIGINS OF THE OBSERVANT MOVEMENT

The Observant movement, which had so great an impact on the friaries of South Germany, was not an indigenous development. The movement began in fourteenth-century Italy. The driving force behind this reform was the desire to return to a closer adherence to the ideal of poverty established by St. Francis. The Observants did not embrace the heritage of the Spirituals. Whether they were, in fact, influenced by the Spirituals is a matter of controversy.

The first community of strict Observants was founded in Brugliano in 1334. By 1335, this group was suppressed by the papacy and the leaders of the order because they insisted on a separatist position within the order and were disobedient to superiors. However, Paul of Trinci, who had lived in the community at Brugliano received permission in 1367 to refound a community of strict observance at the same site. From this time onward, the history of the Observants is continuous.[10] As the movement began to assume control of other houses in the countryside around Brugliano, it was able to emphasize literal keeping of the rule of St. Francis. However, the reformers had not, as yet, explicated rules which would govern the far more complicated life of a friary in a populous city.

The movement spread its influence across the Alps into the French provinces of Burgundy, Tours, and France. It is in this setting that the clearest evidence of a link to the *Fraticelli* has been uncovered. The French Observants appealed in 1415 to the Council of Constance for recognition and partial independence. Livarius Oliger demonstrated that the document presented to the Council of Constance was significantly influenced by the writings of Ubertino of Casale. Ubertino was a leader of the *Fraticelli* at the time of their condemnation by Pope John XXII and eventually joined the circle of supporters of Lewis of Bavaria who urged that the pope be deposed. Although Oliger granted that his study demonstrated only a literary association between the Spirituals of the fourteenth century and the Observants of the fifteenth, he argued that the evidence warranted the conclusion that the writings of Ubertino circulated among the French Observants in the early fifteenth century.[11]

The Council of Constance granted the French Observants permission to establish an order within an order. They were to have their own hierarchy which was partially autonomous from the regular hierarchy of the order. All the Observant houses of a province were to elect their own provincial vicar who was to gain the approval of the Conventual provincial before taking office. The provincial vicars were to choose a general for the Observants who, after confirmation by the general of the order, would serve as his vicar.

The achievement of this partial autonomy was a considerable political triumph for the Observants. They did not win by default, nor was their success due to an exploitation of conciliar-papal conflicts. The Conventuals were there in numbers to oppose the Observants but the latter had the emperor and the French king on their side. This political support was decisive in the outcome of the deliberations.[12]

CHAMPIONS OF THE REFORM

The growth of the Observant movement throughout South Germany did not result from spontaneous adherence to the stricter ideals. Ardent champions of reform were to be found outside the friaries. Popes and bishops, city councils and princes, even the emperor supported the reform. To be sure, there were members of the order who embraced the new regime zealously. On the other hand, resistance to the change was spirited at times.

The initial success of the Observants in South Germany, the reform of Heidelberg in 1426, was a clear case of intervention by the prince. Glassberger, the Observant chronicler, recounted with obvious delight how Louis of the Rhine ordered the reform at the insistence of his wife. Mathilda, from the Piedemont branch of the house of Savoy, had been instructed in her youth by the French Observants of Tours. After discovering that the Heidelberg friary did not meet the standards she had known in Tours, she persuaded her husband to bring French Observants to Heidelberg. Conventual attempts to negate the influence of the reformers only served to arouse Mathilda's wrath. She pressured her husband successfully to insist that the

---

[9] Schmitz, *Der Zustand* . . ., pp. 95–97. For an example of Hussite approval of the Franciscan ideal of poverty see Glassberger, pp. 467–469. One Franciscan chronicle reports that the Hussite influence reached as far as Augsburg where Hussite preachers were permitted activity. See Malachias Tschamser, *Annales oder Jahrs-Geschichten der Baarfüsseren oder Minderen Brudern* (1724), edited by Abbé François-Joseph Merklen (Colmar, 1864) 1, p. 587; hereafter cited as Tschamser.

[10] Moorman, pp. 369–372. *Cf.* Huber, pp. 271–273.

[11] Livarius Oliger, "De Relatione inter Observantium Querimonias Constantienses (1415) et Ubertini Casalensis Quoddam Scriptum," *AFH* 9 (1916): pp. 3–41. *Cf.* Huber, pp. 222, 232 and Franz Ehrle, "Die Spiritualen, ihr Verhältnis zum Franziskanerorden und zu den Fraticellen," *Archiv für Litteratur und Kirchengeschichte des Mittelalters* 4 (1888): pp. 181–190.

[12] Cajetan Schmitz, "Der Anteil der süddeutschen Observantenvikarie an der Durchführung der Reform," *FS* 2 (1915): pp. 364–367. *Cf.* Glassberger, p. 256.

Observants be permitted to complete the reforming task. Not all the friars resisted the reform. Nicolas Caroli, the guardian at Heidelberg, emerged as the local spokesman for the Observants. Within the next several decades he led the reforming delegation which reorganized friary after friary.[13]

The reform of the friary in Nuremberg exemplified the influence of the City Council. The Council appealed to Pope Eugene IV in 1445 that he mandate the reform of the house. The Council complained of spiritual lassitude and internal conflicts between the friends and opponents of the Observants. Eugene ordered the reform specifying that his decision was to supersede any other legal grounds with which the Conventuals might attempt to block the reform. Further, Eugene declared the friary free of obligations to read masses for its benefactors. The properties and income resulting from such agreements were to be turned over to the City Council for reassignment to appropriate charities. Finally, residents of the house who did not wish to live under Observant rules were to be allowed to transfer elsewhere.[14]

A formal ceremony on May 25, 1447, marked the transference of control to the Observants. Present, in addition to the resident friars and their officers, were representatives of the local clergy and four members of the City Council. Nicolas Caroli, now the acknowledged *Custos* of Observants in the province, presided. The keys of the house were taken from the Conventual officers and a new set of Observant officers was installed. The endowment of the house was assigned by the Council to the supervisor of the new hospital. Ornate altarware and robes were inventoried and put away.[15] Thus were the Council's wishes satisfied.

Conflicting evidence exists regarding the impact of the new regime. Glassberger wrote in glowing terms of the prominent new converts attracted to the reformed house. On the other hand, the City Council complained again to Pope Calixtus in 1456 that discipline was lax. Albert Puchelbach, who was the deposed Conventual guardian of the house, reappeared as Observant guardian in 1451.[16]

Within a decade after the reform, severe accusations were made about the house. Apparently the altarware was being sold as a source of income. The guardian was pictured as behaving like a prince or an abbot. His room was outfitted with pillows, curtains and furs. He indulged in the luxury of riding a horse. Women frequented his quarters and his behavior in nunneries was disgraceful. Masses which were supposed to be said in Nuremberg were assigned to other friaries. The guardian was accused of buying favor with the provincial by sending him precious altarware.[17] This period of abuses may have occurred while Puchelbach was absent from Nuremberg (1454–1458). After his return he enjoyed an unblemished reputation as an initiator of Observant reform in nearby houses.[18]

The reform could no more guarantee freedom from the influence of wealthy donors than it could assure the Observants of lofty standards. Three decades after the reform in Nuremberg the walls of the friary still bore the insignia of wealthy families who had contributed to the house and whose forebears were buried there. The Observants attempted in 1469 and again in 1480 to remove these insignia. However, the Waldstromer family, wealthy patricians and benefactors of the house, objected vehemently. Eventually the Waldstromers succeeded, by means of papal intervention, in blocking this part of the Observant purification process.[19]

Still other forces worked to promote the spread of the reform. Duke Lewis called for the reform of Bavarian religious houses in 1464. The Ingolstadt and Landshut friaries were promptly reformed. Only a successful Conventual appeal for papal intervention prevented the total loss of Bavarian houses to the Observants.[20]

In addition, the Council of Basel made the reform of religious houses a part of its program. The reform of the Basel friary in particular was spurred on by the action of the Council.[21] Nicolas Caroli in his statements announcing the reform of the Basel and Nuremberg friaries emphasized strongly that his actions had been authorized by the Council of Basel.[22]

Finally, the Franciscans were not the only order feeling the pressure of reforming zeal. The calls for reforms by princes and the Council of Basel were directed to all orders. Both Basel and Nuremberg experienced the wave of reform in the mid-fifteenth century of which the Franciscans were only a part.[23]

Resistance by the friars to the outside pressures was not pointless. The Conventuals in Frankfurt succeeded in maintaining control of their house. In 1468, a barrage of reform mandates descended on the house. Pope Paul, the archbishop of Mainz, Emperor Frederick, and Duke Frederick all called for the reform of

---

[13] Glassberger, pp. 282–285. See also the author's account in "The Observant Reform Movement in Southern Germany," *Franciscan Studies* 32, Annual 10 (1972): pp. 163, 164.

[14] SAN, 7 farb, Alph., 1859 Urk.

[15] Glassberger, pp. 316–320. A document detailing Caroli's actions reforming the Nuremberg friary is available in the Staatsarchiv in Basel. See SAB, Schwaz, 41.

[16] See the 1451 letter from Capistrano to the guardian Puchelbach in Nuremberg, *AF*, 2: pp. 342, 343.

[17] SAN, S I Lade 103, 2. The date of this document is uncertain and only a few of the accusations are corroborated by other evidence.

[18] Pickel, "Nürnberg," 19 (1913): pp. 9–13.

[19] Glassberger, pp. 440, 441, 471.

[20] Glassberger, pp. 418–422. Cf. Baurreiss, *op. cit.* 5: pp. 68–75.

[21] Wackernagel, "Barfüsserkloster," p. 196.

[22] SAB, Barfüsser-Urkunde, 190. SAB, Schwaz, 41. *Cf. Urkundenbuch der Stadt Basel* 7, edited by Johannes Haller (Basel, 1899): pp. 211–213.

[23] Höss, *op. cit.*, pp. 141–143. See also Wackernagel, *Geschichte* 2, 2: pp. 821–844 and Bauerreiss, *op. cit.* 5: pp. 42 ff. For a discussion of fifteenth-century reform among the Benedictines see Barbara Frank, *Das Erfurter Peterkloster im 15. Jahrhundert*, in: Studien zur Germania Sacra 11 (Göttingen, 1973).

the house.[24] The friars replied that they were indeed willing to observe stricter rules but that they would do so on their own. Transference of control to the Observant hierarchy was not necessary, they insisted.[25] In spite of the powers arrayed against them, the Conventuals retained control.

In other cases, attempted resistance was not successful. In Munich, for instance, papal and princely reform mandates enabled the Observants to take control in spite of bitter Conventual resistance. Friars unreconciled to the new regime transferred to other Conventual houses in Bavaria.[26]

Conventual chroniclers reflected the bitterness of the conflict. They condemned the Observant victories as exercises of raw power. They intimated that the supporters of the Observants were really interested in confiscating friary property. For instance, the City Council of Freiburg was accused of seeking reform of the friary in order to gain control of a forest owned by the house.

The Conventual chroniclers hailed even symbolic resistance. For instance, one noted that after the reform in Pfortzheim the Conventuals marched out proudly with flags flying.[27] Finally, the Conventual chroniclers recorded with a certain glee the closing of many Observant houses by still another surge of reform, the Reformation.[28]

THE ANNIVERSARY MASS

Central to the financial intercourse between friary and town was the anniversary mass. The introduction of the reform required the friary to give up the properties and incomes derived from such masses. There remained the delicate problem of finding a resolution satisfactory to the donor families who were about to lose the spiritual benefits they so earnestly desired.

As an agreement between a friary and citizens, the contract for the anniversary mass was a matter of concern to the city. City officials witnessed and recorded the specific terms of the agreement. Disputes which might arise from real estate transactions involved in such contracts went to city courts.[29] Just as the city saw it as its concern to care for the physical facilities, so also it oversaw the keeping of contracts related to the friaries.

The very point of the mass was that it was to be perpetual. In return for a gift of property or money, the donor family was to be assured that forever in the future all descendants would receive the benefit of prayer for the living as well as the deceased. When the Observant reform disrupted such agreements a settlement had to be achieved which was fair to the friary as well as to the donor. The advocates of reform chose various solutions. The papal authorization of reform in Basel and in Nuremberg freed those friaries from any further obligations to read anniversary masses.[30]

The financial settlement after the reform in Nuremberg was spelled out in detail in a document prepared by those responsible for the reform, among them patricians from the Council. Specific details of the settlement varied from family to family. Some families simply accepted the fact that no special masses would be said for them. In other cases the commitment to continue reading masses regularly was transferred to the nunnery of St. Clare.

Finally the city fathers reported that a number of masses would still be said in the friary. The fruits of these masses were not to be specified for particular families but were to be said for the spiritual benefit of all. Sufficient masses would be said so that spiritual fruit would be available to all who sought it.

This statement, endorsed by laymen, constitutes a most interesting and most important attack on the existence of private masses. Without becoming involved in any sophisticated theological justification of their position the Council committee emphasized the communal character of the celebration of the mass and the benefits to be derived therefrom.[31] In Basel, likewise, the resolution of financial affairs after the reform included the statement that masses would still be read in the friary and that their benefits would be communal, not private.[32]

Although the Council committee was resolving a financial question the theological and ecclesiological overtones are intriguing. The reform of the friary called into question the limited distribution of the fruits of the mass to specific families. The very aristocracy which benefited from the anniversary masses found itself endorsing a more communal concept of the distribution of spiritual benefits.

OBSERVANT IDEALS

Although the Observants engaged in power politics if need dictated, they also enunciated certain higher ideals. First the South German Observants clearly re-

---

[24] SAF, Barfüsser, 1–7. *Cf.* Sigfrid Grän, "Frankfurt/Main," *AFA* **6** (1960): pp. 134–138.

[25] SAF, Barfüsser, 10, 15. The Frankfurt Conventuals were willing to subscribe to the Martinite reform which was popular in North Germany. See Ferdinand Doelle, *Die Martinianische Reformbewegung in der Sächsischen Franziskaner Provinz (Mittel- und Nordostdeutschland) im 15 und 16 Jahrhundert,* in: Franziskanische Studien Beiheft 7 (Münster/W., 1921).

[26] Glassberger, pp. 472, 473. *Cf.* Hueber, 3: cols. 467–470. The fact that the friary in Augsburg remained in Conventual hands was due in part to the Augsburg City Council's policy of not pursuing reform of religious houses with as much vigor as was exhibited by other city councils. See Kiessling, *op. cit.,* pp. 298–300.

[27] Beradus Müller and Victor Tschan, *Chronica de ortu et progressu Almae Provincae Argentinensis ...,* edited by Meinrad Sehi, *AFA* **12** (1964): p. 65; hereafter cited as Müller-Tschan. This chronicle was completed in 1703. See the editor's introduction p. 6.

[28] Tschamser, **1**: p. 563; Müller-Tschan, pp. 85, 131.

[29] See above, ch. II.

[30] SAB. Barfüsser Urkunde, 195: SAN. 7 farb. Alph., 1859 Urk. *Cf. Bullarium Franciscanum,* Nova Series 1, edited by U. Hüntemann (Florence-Quaracchi, 1929), pp. 523, 524.

[31] SAN, 7 farb. Alph. 3159 Urk.

[32] SAB, Schwaz 41; *cf.* SAB, Barfüsser Urkunde 195.

jected the heritage of the Spirituals. Glassberger condemned Lewis of Bavaria, the patron of the Spirituals, for his opposition to the papacy and pictured him as a disloyal son of the church.[33] Moreover the Observant rhetoric was practical and specific in outlook, never achieving the cosmic dimensions of the Spirituals.[34]

The Observant program for the entire order at the time of the Council of Constance was described by Luke Wadding. The Observant was expected to preach to the people regularly. Bernardine of Siena and John of Capistrano were the shining examples of this dictum.

This public activity was to be accompanied by arduous cultivation of the friars' own spirituality. Vigils, prayers, and fasts of a most strenuous duration were demanded. To facilitate the preservation of the purest form of chastity, the friars were to avoid conversation with women. Finally, strict poverty was to be observed.[35]

John of Capistrano, the famous preacher and ardent Observant, wrote the guardian of the Nuremberg friary in 1452 describing the training which should be given those novices who had joined the order as a result of Capistrano's preaching in Leipzig and who had been sent to Nuremberg for their initial training. Capistrano commanded a strict novitiate. The friar chosen to oversee the novices, Capistrano insisted, should be a man of unblemished character. Nothing should be asked of the novices which had not yet been achieved by the overseer. The novices should, above all else, devote time to meditation on their own sinfulness and need for repentance.

Even though the friar was to exercise a public ministry, the laity were not to be allowed in the friary. In particular, Capistrano emphasized that no laity should be permitted at meals. He commented that the friary need not fear that such rules would estrange the public. Quite the contrary, the reputation of strict holiness would do far more, Capistrano promised, to draw converts and lay support to the friary.[36]

In sum, the Observant regime was a combination of that of the friary and the monastery. The Observant movement did not give up the goal of a public ministry to the city but it did require that considerable time be devoted to private spirituality as well as to separation from the world in the earlier tradition of monasticism.

THE PREACHING OF ST. JOHN OF CAPISTRANO

Historical records bear little evidence of the ministry carried on by the average friar. Considerable attention was devoted to the unusual and the great. Among Franciscan preachers such was John of Capistrano.

In the mid-fifteenth century, Capistrano wandered throughout the South German Province preaching repentance to all the people and calling for the reform of his order. The impact of his preachings was immense. He was no simple wandering friar who appeared uninvited to remonstrate with the people in the marketplace. In both Frankfurt and Nuremberg the City Council extended an official welcome to the famous preacher.

Capistrano's magnetism was all the more astonishing when one considers that he preached in Latin and that a colleague translated his words to the assembled crowds. As a part of his call to repentance, Capistrano urged the burning of the vanities. Chess boards, dice, and expensive clothing would be gathered together and burnt in a symbolic bonfire of repentance.

In addition, Capistrano was famed for his power to heal the sick. Employing holy relics associated with his predecessor and former colleague, St. Bernardine of Siena, Capistrano was hailed as the healer of hundreds. In both Frankfurt and Nuremberg, a list of those healed by this saint was drawn up to attest to his spiritual power.[37]

But Capistrano had a more specific task than to call the people to repentance and to heal their illnesses. He sought to lead the Hussites back to the fold and to rally support for the papal crusade against the Turks. As a man of diplomatic skills together with high moral repute, Capistrano was called upon to mediate political disputes and bring peace to those cities in which he preached. For instance, during his visit to Nuremberg in 1452, he unsuccessfully attempted to mediate a dispute between the City Council and Margrave Albrecht of Ansbach.[38]

In spite of the fact that Capistrano was granted a position of eminence by most contemporaries, he was not without his detractors. The faculties of universities gave him a cool reception. In Erfurt one such faculty member questioned the validity of his miracles.[39] Glassberger found it necessary to defend Capistrano against charges that he was overzealous in search of glory and money. Further, Glassberger engaged in special pleading regarding the validity of his miracles.[40]

An additional charge made in more modern times regarding St. John of Capistrano is that his preaching encouraged the anti-Semitic attitudes of the populace in late medieval cities. There are several references to Capistrano's participation in attacks on the Jewish population in Italy before his tours to Germany. He

---

[33] Glassberger, pp. 133, 134. By the early fifteenth century, the threat of such groups as Beguines and Beghards to the orthodoxy and order of the friars had also diminished. For a description of the suppression of the Beguines in Basel in the early fifteenth century see Brigitte Degler-Spengler, "Die Beginnen in Basel," *Basler Zeitschrift für Geschichte und Altertumskunde* **69** (1969): pp. 5–83; **70** (1970): pp. 29–118.

[34] For a discussion of the scope of reform ideas current among the Spirituals, see Ernst Benz, *Ecclesia Spiritualis: Kirchenidee und Geschichtstheologie der franziskanischen Reformation* (Stuttgart, 1934).

[35] *AM*, **9**: pp. 386, 387.

[36] *AF*, **2**: pp. 242, 243.

[37] Johannes Hofer, *Johannes Kapistran* (2 v., Heidelberg, 1964) **2**: pp. 44–51, 153. *Cf.* Strauss, *Nuremberg*, pp. 210, 211, and Grän, *op. cit.*, pp. 132, 133.

[38] Hofer, *op. cit.* **2**: pp. 149–154.

[39] *Ibid.*, pp. 167, 168.

[40] Glassberger, pp. 336, 337.

was responsible for the enforcement of papal legislation which forbade the Jewish population to have social intercourse with Christians or to hold office. Further, Capistrano was credited with having been so overwhelming in his presentation of the Christian side in a disputation against a Roman rabbi that the rabbi converted and led many followers with him to Christianity.[41]

While on his preaching tours of Germany, Capistrano urged the strict enforcement of legislation segregating the Jewish population from any intercourse with Christians. Pogroms against the Jewish population dogged Capistrano's footsteps throughout Eastern Europe. While the extent to which Capistrano was directly responsible for such actions may be debatable, he surely cannot be absolved of all responsibility for the tragedies.[42] Some of the zeal of the Observants spilled over into hostility against the non-Christian minority.

RESOLUTION OF THE CONFLICT

By the first years of the sixteenth century, the Observant-Conventual conflict was an open scandal. Clamorous accusations were made that friaries had been stolen by one side or the other. Ecclesiastical courts ruled on some disputed cases while the emperor and kings called for an end to the struggle.

By the turn of the century the Observants controlled fifteen houses. Pressure for reform continued—witness the forced reform of Freiburg in 1514. Controlling influential houses and basking in the favor of powerful friends, the Observants had become a dominant force in the province.

In the midst of this chaotic turmoil the South German Observants elected a new provincial vicar. From his election in 1514 onward, Caspar Schatzgeyer, formerly an officer of Observant houses in Ingolstadt and Munich, was the spokesman for the Observant cause. His *Apologia* published in 1516 was an unqualified defense of Observant tactics. Observant disobedience to authorities was excused as a necessary evil resulting from the search for perfect obedience to the rule of St. Francis. All of the enmity and scandal, the harsh expulsion of Conventual friars from the newly reformed houses as well as the intervention of the political arm on behalf of the Observants were excused as means toward the glorious end. The Observant actions were not merely excusable; they were lauded as worthy of the eternal reward. Conventuals who failed to understand this were labeled pharisees in contrast with the Christ-like Observants. The document was thoroughly haughty and unforgiving.[43]

Schatzgeyer also indulged himself in the actual exercise of Observant power. Both the pope and emperor had called for the reform of the Freiburg friary but the Conventual party in the house was firm in its resistance. Schatzgeyer was deputized by the papal legate, Campeggio, to deliver the reforming bull to the house. Thus was the reform forced on an unwilling constituency.[44]

A general chapter of the order was assembled in Rome in 1517 to resolve the dispute. The obstinacy on both sides prevented any harmonious solution. Instead, the papal documents issued after the meeting institutionalized the split within the order. The parties were insolated from interference in each others' affairs but the principal chain of command was taken from the Conventuals and given to the Observants. The Observants were triumphant but the unity of the order was abandoned in theory as well as practice.[45]

OUTCOMES

The strictures of Observant life did not lead to a decline in the influence of reformed friaries. Quite the contrary, the reformed houses were renowned not only for their spirituality but for their intellectual ferment as well. It was the Strassburg friary, one of the most prominent Conventual houses, which experienced a serious decline in numbers and wealth in the late fifteenth century. By contrast, the Nuremberg house flourished in the years immediately after it was reformed. Its ranks were swelled by numerous neophytes many of them of influential rank in the city.[46]

The reform was not, however, an unmixed success. Since the Observants did not return to absolute poverty, a certain ambiguity regarding financial support remained. Financial records indicate that certain pious endowments were still accepted by reformed houses.[47]

Further, the Observants regularly faced the criticism that they were overzealous in their pursuit of power and esteem. This charge stemmed from the nature of the Observant—Conventual struggle. In the last decades before the definitive settlement of the struggle, there were several unsightly examples of dual claim to control over friaries. When one hierarchy fought with another, reformist ideals seemed to fade in the face of sheer power politics.[48]

What was worse, the Observant position smacked of intolerable pride. Promotion of rigorous ideals implied regular pejorative comparisons with Conventuals. John

---

[41] *AM*, **11**: pp. 322–326; **12**: p. 74.

[42] Hofer, *op. cit.* **2**: pp. 221–228. *Cf.* Cecil Roth, *The Jews in the Renaissance* (Philadelphia, 1959), p. 14. The virulent anti-Semitism of this period was well represented in other sources. The chronicle recalling affairs in the friary of Thann in Alsace contains vivid accounts of pogroms against Jews in retaliation for their alleged desecration of the host or holy week attacks on Christian children. See Tschamser, **1**: pp. 641, 642, 684, 693, 694, 732.

[43] Caspar Schatzgeyer, *Apologia status fratrum ordinis minorum de Observantia nuncupatorum declaratorio* (Basel, 1516). *Cf.* the author's "The Observant Reform Movement in Southern Germany," pp. 158–160. For a biography of Schatzgeyer see Nikolaus Paulus, *Kaspar Schatzgeyer, Ein Vorkämpfer der katholischen Kirche gegen Luther in Süddeutschland*, in: Strassburger Theologische Studien 3, 1 (Strassburg, 1898).

[44] Paulus, *op. cit.*, pp. 30–33.

[45] Moorman, pp. 569–585.

[46] Glassberger pp. 318–320 and Hueber, 3: cols. 452–455. *Cf.* Stahl, *op. cit.*, pp. 130–154.

[47] Pickel, "Nürnberg," **19** (1913): pp. 21, 22.

[48] Huber, pp. 459–470.

Pauli, a Strassburg Conventual, complained that of all the scourges of the regular clergy, the Observants were the worst. Behind their boastful posture was emptiness. They spoke of poverty but did not know the pinch of real need. Humility was on their lips but they would accept remonstrance from none.[49] Their avid pursuit of a modest goal made the Observants an easy target for scorn.

By the end of the fifteenth century, the Observants were no longer militant insurgents. They were now entrenched and established, eager to maintain the status quo. The affair of Casper Waler clearly illustrated the Observant mood.

Waler came to prominence in Bavaria in 1485 as a proponent of strict poverty. He utilized the same slogans and tactics which had earlier served the Observants so well. Now it was the Observants who spoke of the need for peace. Reassertions of poverty ideals were issued by the Observants but they were far too guarded for Waler. For example, the Observants proceeded to define acceptable kinds of gifts to friaries. Just this sort of compromise was the object of his attack. The last years of the controversy saw Waler disciplined in one house in the Province only to emerge elsewhere with his aggressive program. The Observants' attempt to cope with him made them look strangely like Conventuals.[50]

Finally, the way in which the reform was carried out strengthened the hand of city councils and princes in their control of the friaries. The movement which sought to free the houses from entanglements with secular riches provided a powerful precedent for political intervention in friary affairs. As long as such intervention sought to promote the welfare of the houses, it provided no occasion for comment. But the friars were fatally vulnerable to a less benign intervention by princes and city councils.[51]

IV. THE INTELLECTUAL HABIT

The friars' participation in the world of learning increased markedly as the sixteenth century began. Prominent friars moved in humanist circles. By attending universities, they obtained a broader education than that offered by friary schools. Their names were associated as authors and editors with humanist publications. Increasingly they defined their ministry to society in terms of teaching and writing.

THE FIFTEENTH CENTURY

Although the provincial chronicles began to boast of intellectual achievements in the late fifteenth century, the order was not without men of letters earlier in the century. For example, John Grütsch, the holder of a doctorate, was a renowned preacher in Basel early in the century. Later printed editions of his sermons proved to be popular.[1]

Formal education in friary schools became more readily obtainable during the fifteenth century. Since the early fourteenth century, Strassburg alone had the authority to offer *studium generale*. In 1448 the Nuremberg friary also received permission to give instruction in *studium generale*.[2] Then in 1471 the provincial capital approved a much wider distribution of schools throughout the province. Theology was to be taught in the friaries of Basel, Ingolstadt, and Heidelberg while liberal arts were to be pursued in Mainz, Bamberg, and Heilbron.[3] Even in friaries with no special authorization lively intellectual activity was possible. Conrad Pellican, a prominent humanist among the Franciscans, recalled the eager pursuit of theology and humanistic subjects at Tübingen in the last years of the century.[4] It was not by accident that the best chronicle history of the province in the late Middle Ages—Glassberger's—was written in the Nuremberg friary. The pursuit of letters had flourished there for a century before Glassberger wrote. An inventory of the friary library taken in 1448 recorded a rich variety of literature on hand. For the study of the Bible, guidance was available from the commentaries of Jerome, Augustine, Gregory, and even Nicholas of Lyra. Scholastic theology was well represented by volumes of Anselm and Aquinas, Bonaventura and Duns Scotus, Holcott and Bradwardine, together with many others. Editions of canon law were available. But the studious friar was not limited to later medieval authors. Augustine, Jerome, Origen, and Ambrose represented the fathers. Likewise works of Boethius and Cassiodorus were to be found. Classical literature was represented by Ovid and Aristotle, the Renaissance by Petrarch and Boccaccio. Finally, treatises on medicine by Galen, Hippocrates, and Constantine the African were included. The friar possessing an interest in letters had rich resources at hand.[5] Not only were the resources available, but there are reports of scientific and humanist studies carried on in the friary, particularly instruction in the use of the astrolabe.[6]

Since the founding of the order the pursuit of learning held an ambiguous position, suspect in theory but in practice ardently cultivated by many friars. Although the Observants had a reputation in some quarters as enemies of learning, such hostility was not manifest in South Germany. On the contrary, with the exception of Strassburg, the Observants, not the Con-

---

[49] Johannes Pauli, *Schimpf und Ernst*, edited by Johannes Bolte, in: Alte Erzähler 1 (Berlin, 1924): p. 14.
[50] Hueber. 3: cols. 507–520; Glassberger, pp. 515–518; Cajetan Schmitz, "Der Anteil der süddeutschen Observantenvikarie," pp. 373–376.
[51] For a discussion of the impact of lay interest in ecclesiastical reform and humanist learning on the church in late medieval Augsburg see Kiessling, *op. cit.*, pp. 306–315.

[1] Eubel, *Geschichte*, p. 35.
[2] Rapp, *op. cit.*, pp. 12, 13; Stahl, *op. cit.*, p. 136.
[3] Glassberger, pp. 450, 451.
[4] See below, pp. 18, 19.
[5] *Mittelalterliche Bibliothekskataloge Deutschlands und der Schweiz* 3, 3, edited by Paul Ruf (Munich, 1939): pp. 752–765.
[6] Ulrich Schmidt, *Das ehemalige Franziskaner-Kloster in Nürnberg* (Nuremberg, 1913), p. 50.

ventuals, led the intellectual life of the province at the end of the century.[7]

Further, the friars offered education not only to their own but to local children as well. Two prominent sixteenth-century leaders of the order—Conrad Pellican and Casper Schatzgeyer—were first associated with the order as pupils in friary schools.[8]

By the turn of the century intellectual prowess earned prestige in the order. The chronicles provide glowing accounts of disputations on philosophical and theological topics before packed audiences at provincial capitals. One account took special delight in noting that provincial capitals were attended by theologians familiar with the currents of Parisian thought.[9] The provincial capital of 1502 was attended by five friars holding doctorates. Beginning in 1483 the office of provincial was controlled for four decades by holders of that degree.[10]

THE HIGH TIDE OF LEARNING 1500–1517

Beginning in 1501, a Mariological dispute between Franciscans and Dominicans raged through the province, stirring up the feelings of laity as well as clergy. The debate began in Heidelberg when the Dominicans attacked the Franciscan teaching of the Immaculate Conception of Mary. A disputation was scheduled but the prince of the Pfalz refused to allow it, fearing that it would create too much uproar among the people. The Franciscan provincial answered that it should be held although he granted that the common people should not be allowed to attend. The dispute later spread to Frankfurt where, according to Glassberger's report, it evoked riotous crowds.

The Dominicans in Bern were so determined to drive their Franciscan opponents out of town that they claimed miracles had been sent to vindicate their position. Mary and other saints had appeared in their house, they declared. At first the reports attracted the desired popular acclaim. But as the evidence mounted that the claims were fraudulent, popular opinion turned against the Dominicans, the City Council instigated an investigation, and eventually the perpetuators of the fraud were executed.[11]

Still more evidence of the rapport between the friars and the people was provided by the collection of sermon and anecdotes published by John Pauli. An admirer of the great preacher Geiler of Kaisersberg, Pauli published his folksy *Schimpf Und Ernst* so that preachers might be able to wake up their audiences and the regular clergy might enjoy jovial relaxation amidst the stern discipline of their houses.[12] These simple anecdotes referred to the daily routine of the marketplace. They told of the reactions of farm animals as parables of human behavior and they mocked the petty conflicts of marriage and family life. But interspersed with these humble tales were quotations from the fathers and the scholastics. One hears also echoes of humanists such as Petrarch. This collection of folk wisdom with its learned overtones was widely read during the next two centuries.[13]

FRIARS AND HUMANISTS: PELLICAN AND MURNER

The swelling tide of humanism ripped open new fissures in the cultural life of Europe. The happy wedding of letters and obedience was no longer possible. The developing tension was illustrated by the careers of two friars of the province, Conrad Pellican and Thomas Murner.

Both of these friars pursued humanist learning while wearing the friar's habit. Both employed their talents as editor and author to reach that eager, literate audience beyond the circle of fellow friars. Each in his own way was critical of the theology and morals of the clergy.

In his autobiographical chronicle Pellican emphasized the point that his education had been thoroughly Franciscan. Taught as a child in the friary school in his home village in Alsace, he joined the order in 1493 in part, at least, because his family could not pay for his university education. From the very first, Pellican viewed life in the order as an opportunity to pursue learning as well as piety.

Pellican encountered his beloved mentor, Paul Scriptoris, when he was sent to the Tübingen friary. In his chronicle, written from the perspective of Protestant Zurich, Pellican sought to picture Scriptoris as a "Reformer before the Reformation." Even if this desire to make a Reformer out of Scriptoris is to be rejected as unhistorical, there is an historical kernel to be found in Pellican's recollections of his teacher.[14]

---

[7] For a discussion of St. Francis's distrust of erudition see Rosalind B. Brooke, *Early Franciscan Government* (Cambridge, 1959), pp. 84, 85. Hofer described Capistrano as afraid of "heathen humanism" but an advocate of "Christian humanism." See Hofer, *op. cit.* 1: pp. 323–329. For examples of Observant critiques of overemphasis on learning see Moorman, pp. 534–536.

[8] For Pellican see his *Das Chronikon des Konrad Pellikan*, edited by Bernhard Riggenbach (Basel, 1877), pp. 9, 10; hereafter cited as Pellican, *Chronikon*. For Schatzgeyer see John Bachmann's introduction to Schatzgeyer's posthumously published *Opera Omnia* (Ingolstadt, 1543).

[9] Tschamser, 1: pp. 702, 703. The Müller-Tschan account of late fifteenth-century provincial capitals is included in part one of the Chronicle. Unfortunately part one was omitted from the text published in *AFA*. The entire Chronicle is available in typescript in the Würzburg Universitäts-Bibliothek, edited by Meinrad Sehi (Würzburg, 1957). For the account of the provincial capitals see 1: p. 65.

[10] Theodor von Liebenau, *Der Franziskaner Dr. Thomas Murner*, in: Erläuterungen und Ergänzungen zu Janssens Geschichte des deutschen Volkes 9, 4/5 (Freiburg/Br., 1913): p. 21; hereafter cited as Liebenau. Müller-Tschan, pp. 289, 290.

[11] Glassberger, pp. 526–528. Hueber, 3: cols. 539–549. See also Georg Schuhmann, *Die Berner Jetzertragodie im Lichte der neueren Forschung und Kritik*, in: Erläuterungen und Ergänzungen zu Janssens Geschichte des deutschen Volkes 4, 3 (Freiburg/Br., 1912).

[12] See the Bolte introduction to Pauli, *op cit.*, pp. 7–16.

[13] *Ibid.*, pp. 22–25. See also Eubel, *Geschichte*, pp. 66–67.

[14] Pellican, *Chronikon*, pp. 10–16. See also the author's "Caspar Schatzgeyer and Conrad Pellican: The Triumph of

Although he was trained in theology at the University of Paris, Scriptoris did not limit his instruction to the strict confines of scholastic theology. He studied Greek and corresponded with Reuchlin. Young friars at Tübingen were instructed in a broad range of liberal arts. His pupils studied Ptolemy and Euclid and became familiar with the use of the astrolabe.

But most important is Pellican's report that Scriptoris had become a theological dissident. He urged Pellican to turn away from the scholastics and to go back to the early church fathers to find the pure sources of Christian teaching. The teachings of Scriptoris aroused the suspicions of the theologians at the University of Tübingen. At their instigation, an investigation was begun. As a result, Scriptoris was stripped of his position as guardian in Tübingen and was sent to Basel with prohibitions against his further teaching or preaching.[15]

Pellican's return to the sources took him back beyond even the fathers of the early Church to the study of the Hebrew background to Christianity. While a child, he had been impressed by the difficulty a Christian had experienced in debating with a Jewish scholar. As he began his theological studies, he observed that difficult exegetical problems could not be solved without a return to the original language. Therefore, he set out to learn Hebrew. Since his days were filled with the required study of scholastic theology, it was at night that he found time to pursue Hebrew. Although Scriptoris and Reuchlin encouraged and assisted him, Hebrew grammars, dictionaries and documents were not readily available. Pellican utilized every opportunity to obtain materials and enter into conversation with those learned in Hebrew including Jewish scholars.[16]

In spite of the action taken against Scriptoris, his prize pupil was appointed *lector* in the Basel friary in 1502. The appointment was, indeed, appropriate. Humanist learning flourished in the friary just as it abounded in the city. In the friary, Pellican enjoyed as a colleague Franz Wiler, a talented preacher, musician, and poet. Wiler was one of many regular clergy who had assisted the Amerbach publishing house in an ambitious program of publication of the great ecclesiastical authors. Wiler perpared an edition of Bonventura and assisted in the preparation of the edition of Augustine. Also prominent in the friary were Daniel Agricola, the editor of Lombard, and Frederich Kraft, an expert in the use of the astrolabe. Sebastian Brant honored still another friar, John Meder, by dedicating one of his works to him.[17]

Pellican joined a long line of regular clergy who assisted the Amerbach house in publishing editions of the fathers. In this circle Pellican encountered, in addition to Wiler, men such as Conrad of Leonberg, a Cistercian, who was the principal editor of the Augustine edition. Over two decades, Pellican helped see editions of Augustine, Tertullian, Jerome, and Cyprian through the press. In the course of his researches, Pellican came to doubt the authenticity of certain writings attributed to early church fathers. For example, he questioned the attribution of *De vera et falsa penitentia* to Augustine. Although Pellican entertained such doubts in 1505, the Amerbach edition of Augustine, which appeared in 1505 and 1506, contained this treatise without any special comment. It was Erasmus who in 1522 committed himself in print to the assertion that this treatise was not an authentic work of Augustine's. Patristic studies led Pellican to doubt that a number of tenets of scholastic theology could be supported from the fathers. He mentioned such teachings as indulgences, purgatory, penance, papal power and transubstantiation as dogmas which seemed to have little currency in the early church.

From 1514 to 1517 Pellican was the traveling companion and assistant to Schatzgeyer, the provincial vicar of South German Franciscans. The major task of these two men was to travel the length and breadth of the province visiting all the friaries. Pellican utilized this visitation tour to search for documents and contact other scholars who could aid his Hebrew studies. Among others he visited Nicholas Ellenbog in the monastery at Ottobeuren and Abbot Trithemius of Sponheim in order to consult their Hebrew collections. John Eck in Ingolstadt and Charitas Pirckheimer in Nuremberg also assisted his research. As his career continued, it was increasingly the pursuit of Hebrew and Old Testament exegesis which became Pellican's specialty. In fact, by 1526 when he joined Zwingli in Zurich, he came as a professor of Hebrew and Old Testament.

Finally, one should note Pellican's reaction to a journey to Rome to participate in the important Chapter General of the order in 1517 when the Observants triumphed. Regarding the central purpose of the journey Pellican made only a few comments. He suggested that the Observants had won a great victory because they paid the pope huge sums of money. Appropriately impressed with Italy as the homeland of St. Francis, he also marveled at the many magnificent churches he saw there. While traveling as an officer of his province, Pellican regularly looked beyond the affairs of the friars to pursue his intellectual interests.[18]

Although Thomas Murner was accepted into the Conventual house in Strassburg at age fifteen in 1490,

---

Dissension in the Early Sixteenth Century," *Archiv für Reformationsgeschichte* **61** (1970): pp. 180, 181.

[15] Pellican, *Chronikon*, pp. 13–23.

[16] *Ibid.*, pp. 15–21. The efforts of Pellican to promote Semitic studies were crowned with success in the career of his pupil, Sebastian Münster. See Karl Heinz Burmeister, *Sebastian Münster: Versuch eines biographischen Gesamtbildes*, in: Basler Beiträge zur Geschichtswissenschaft **93** (Basel, 1963).

[17] Wackernagel, *Geschichte* **3**: pp. 138–141. *Cf.* Pellican, *Chronikon,* pp. 26, 27 and *Die Amerbachkorrespondenz,* edited by Alfred Hartmann (2 v., Basel, 1942–1943) **1**: pp. 151–153, 185, 186, 193, 194, 199–201.

[18] See the author's "Caspar Schatzgeyer and Conrad Pellican ...," pp. 184–190. *Cf. Die Amerbachkorrespondenz* **1**: pp. 137, 138, 177–181, 357, 358.

he received his education as an itinerant student visiting prominent universities such as Paris, Freiburg, Cologne, Vienna, and Basel. His father was said to have paid six hundred gulden as the price of this extensive education. As a symbol of Murner's loose relation to the order, he sometimes wore the clothes of a layman.[19]

Even more than Pellican, Murner was actively involved in the study of topics outside theology. Interested in philosophical logic, he was famous for his ability to teach the subject very quickly illustrating basic principles to his pupils by the use of card games. He studied Latin literature and law although Ulrich Zasius, the eminent jurist of Freiburg, expressed grave reservations regarding Murner's competence in the latter area.[20] Finally, he was a prolific writer, first as a satirist of the church and its morals and later of the Reformers, whom he saw as agents of the devil himself.

Murner's attempt to be a humanist in Franciscan habit was challenged by the leading humanist of Strassburg, Jacob Wimpfeling, who was, incidentally, a friend of Murner's father. The younger Murner had returned to Strassburg in 1501, after his student years, to become friary preacher. He quickly cultivated a friendship with Wimpfeling receiving an invitation from the humanist to use his library. However, both men had exalted ideas of their own intellectual achievements and it soon became clear that there was not room for both of them in the same city.

In 1501 Wimpfeling published his *Germania,* an attempt to establish himself as a spokesman for the new learning in Strassburg. The first part of the book was devoted to insisting that the empire had always been German, not French in character, and that Strassburg, a German city, was an integral part of the empire. The second part of this publication contained barbs directed against Murner and other clergy. Wimpfeling suggested that the city fathers should establish a school for the education of Strassburg youth because of the inadequacies of the ecclesiastical education presently being provided. His comments reflected directly on the friary school with which Murner was associated.

Murner took up the challenge promptly. He contended that the French heritage had been unjustly maligned by his opponent. Much ink was spilled over the question of French versus German elements in the medieval imperial tradition. However, the crux of the issue for Murner was the question of the quality of ecclesiastical education. As a representative of the ecclesiastical tradition, but one who considered himself every inch a man of letters, Murner would not tolerate Wimpfeling's condescension. This question finally evolved into a discussion of the intellectual achievement of monks in history. Augustine had become a symbol of monastic learnedness but Wimpfeling insisted that Augustine never was a monk. In these terms the two debated the question about the setting of education. Could it go on in traditional ecclesiastical surroundings or did the humanist spirit require that it be freed from that environment? In spite of Wimpfeling's protests, the humanists never did succeed in establishing their city school in Strassburg.[21]

The side effects of the controversy were immense. Wimpfeling recruited his friends as active opponents of Murner, thus estranging the friar from the humanist circles of Strassburg. The City Council meanwhile feared conflict between the French and German communities. Since Wimpfeling's *Germania* had already received the Council's acclaim as a song of praise to the city, Murner's belligerence was resented. Hence, the Council forbade further publication of Murner's writings dealing with this controversy. Thus the Council initiated a policy of censorship to which it resorted frequently during the Reformation.[22]

The bitter outcome of the conflict with Wimpfeling did not diminish Murner's appetite for controversy or for humanist efforts. He was named poet laureate by Emperor Maximilian in 1505 in spite of the fact that none of his greater literary efforts had appeared by that time. Apparently the honor was given in recognition of his attempts to put classical literature in the service of theology. His acceptance of the award was approved by the general of the order.[23]

Murner's first great work was written in Bern where he had been sent in 1509 to help revitalize the friary. Murner selected the Dominicans who had perpetrated the fraudulent miracles as objects of his satire. In a long, moralistic poem entitled, *Von den vier ketzeren Prediger,* Murner recounted the events which led up to the execution of the Dominicans. Although there has been considerable controversy over the accuracy of Murner's description of events, the moral lessons he wished to draw are quite clear. First of all, the action of the Dominicans was a terrible heresy and deserved harsh punishment. In addition, he called on the reader at the end of his work to honor Mary as immaculately conceived. The grotesque heresy of the Dominicans was juxtaposed with the spiritual beauty of the Franciscan teaching. Murner seized upon the bizarre affair as an opportunity to win debating points in the perennial conflict between the two orders.[24]

The attractiveness of Murner's intellectual capabilities together with the unattractiveness of his personality kept him moving frequently. In 1511 he went to Frankfurt to serve as preacher. There for a brief

---

[19] Liebenau, pp. 8–15.
[20] Adalbert Erler, *Thomas Murner als Jurist* (Frankfurt, 1956), pp. 22, 23.
[21] Waldemar Kawerau, *Thomas Murner und die Kirche des Mittelalters,* in: Schriften des Vereins für Reformationsgeschichte **30** (Halle, 1890): pp. 26–35.
[22] *Ibid.,* p. 29, Liebenau, pp. 27, 28.
[23] Liebenau, pp. 36–40.
[24] "Von den vier ketzeren Prediger" edited by Eduard Fuchs in: *Thomas Murners Deutsche Schiften* (Berlin, 1929) 1, 1: pp. 157–160.

time, he achieved great success in establishing himself as the leading religious intellectual of the town. Employing a style frequently compared with that of Geiler of Kaisersberg, Murner called for reform, harping especially on the morals of the clergy. In a powerful satire *Die Schelmenzunft* published during his Frankfurt years, Murner displayed this critical style. In one chapter for example, he mocked the canon lawyers. They were pictured as slaves of their legal forms, motivated by no higher goal than the desire for money. Only when they had been well paid would they produce legal briefs, marvelously inscribed and sealed. But without payment they refused to do anything. Large audiences flocked to hear his sermons.[25]

While in Frankfurt, Murner found himself embroiled in the controversy between Reuchlin and Pfefferkorn regarding the use of Hebrew documents. Although there is no direct statement from Murner supporting Reuchlin's position, it appears that he was closely identified with Reuchlin's side of the controversy. First, he had a reputation as a great opponent of the Dominicans because of his activities in Bern. Further, he was mentioned in the *Epistolae Obscurorum Virorum* as a supporter of Reuchlin.[26] Finally, in 1512 he published a selection of Jewish prayers in translation. Although the quality of the translation does not say much for the depth of his knowledge of Hebrew, it does appear that in this fashion he symbolically indicated his approval of the use of Hebrew materials. Of course, this action enhanced his reputation as a man of letters.[27]

Both Pellican and Murner were dealing with Jewish documents during the time of the Reuchlin controversy. Pellican's Chronicle is remarkable for its freedom from attack on the Jewish tradition. Pellican eagerly sought Hebrew documents and assistance from Jewish scholars. He did not add any disparaging remarks in his Chronicle about the Jewish religious tradition but rather saved his satire for the Dominicans in Ratisbon who would not allow one of their own to make a copy of a Talmudic lexicon for Pellican lest the copyist be polluted in the process.[28] Murner, on the other hand, made frequent disparaging references to the Jewish religious tradition in his writings, often using the Jew as the symbol of heresy and religious ignorance.[29]

Finally, during his Frankfurt years, Murner justified the confidence which the emperor had previously invested in his literary abilities. In addition to the *Schelmenzunft*, he published in 1512 his *Narrenbeschwörung*. In this work, Murner took the theme of the fool which had been developed by Sebastian Brant and reworked the idea in a radically religious fashion.

One could, in fact, say that in this work Murner used the tools of the humanist to express the message of the late medieval preacher.

In Brant's *Narrenschiff* the author was essentially a moral preacher. The fool was presented as the man who was intellectually, morally, and religiously blind. He did not understand, he did not grasp values nor did he see his own sin. By exposing the fool to the intellect of the reader, Brant sought to teach wisdom and morality to his own audience.

Murner had a far more religious conception of the fool. The fool in Murner's writings was not merely blind, he was positively evil. Far from failing merely to comprehend moral values, he was the enemy of moral values. The concept of *Beschwörung* pointed in the direction of the diabolical and the demonic. The fool was, in Murner's presentation, finally in the grip of the power of sin and of Satan. The solution to the dilemma of foolish humanity was then very different for Murner than it was for Brant. If Brant's fool needed enlightenment, Murner's fool needed salvation. Only by a religious rebirth could man be freed from captivity to the sinful and the demonic. Mere enlightenment, heightened moral understanding was insufficient.[30]

In these writings, Murner achieved the highest point of his career as a Franciscan humanist. Exhibiting a powerful command of literary techniques and speaking within a tradition revered among humanist authors, Murner faithfully reproduced the message of the mendicant preacher.

CONCLUSION

Historians are wont to contrast the new learning with the old, the humanist with the scholastic. Indeed Pellican reinforced this disjunction by his disdainful description of the sterile pursuit of Scotism among his colleagues. He implied that during his own youth the required hours of study of scholastic authors inhibited his purusit of humanist topics.[31]

In fact the humanistic learning had its medieval roots. Both Pauli and Murner drew on the literary style of the mendicant preacher. The scholars of the early sixteenth century boasted of their knowledge of Biblical languages and their pursuit of scientific topics. Still, Lyra and Galen were to be found in the Nuremberg friary a century before them.

It was not new topics of study but new settings in which learning was being pursued which caused the crisis in the order. Faithfulness to the rule of St. Francis had been measured according to the standard of poverty.[32] But while the order was in uproar over the question of poverty, quite another problem was surfacing. Success in the society of humanistic *literati*

---

[25] "Die Schelmenzunft" edited by M. Spanier in *Thomas Murners Deutsche Schriften* (Berlin, 1925) **3**: pp. 51–53. *Cf.* Liebenau, pp. 68, 69.

[26] *Epistolae Obscurorum Virorum*, edited by Francis Griffin Stokes (London, 1925), pp. 136, 137.

[27] Liebenau, pp. 72–77.

[28] See the author's "Caspar Schatzgeyer and Conrad Pellican...," pp. 188, 189.

[29] Liebenau, pp. 77, 78.

[30] Barbara Könneker, *Wesen und Wandlung der Narrenidee im Zeitalter des Humanismus. Brant, Murner, Erasmus* (Wiesbaden, 1966), pp. 133–180.

[31] Pellican, *Chronikon*, p. 18.

[32] Moorman, pp. 12–17.

was alienating prominent friars from the discipline of the order.

The locus of Murner's actvity was controlled, at least as much, by city councils and other humanists as it was by his superiors in the order. Likewise, Pellican seized a role in an intellectual community totally outside the discipline of the order. The very success of these two gifted men made them something other than humble friars.

This acceptance of the humanist's role violated the intentions of St. Francis. His rejection of wealth was not an end in itself. Rather it was a way of preventing his followers from taking up the selfish pursuit of prestige and power.[33] The guardian who lived like a wealthy abbot was not the only threat to the observance of the rule. Renaissance cities eagerly competed for the wits of leading humanists. The humanists, in turn, sought after the influence and prestige given to famous men of letters. The roles of friar and humanist came increasingly into conflict in the first two decades of the century. The fateful third decade put an end to comfortable evasions.

V. YEARS OF CONFUSION, 1517–1522

No task is more difficut for students of the Reformation than that of becoming a genuine contemporary of those who saw the first events of this great upheaval. For us the extent of the revolt and the issues involved are clearly defined. All of this was far from clear to those who lived through those years.

The Franciscans in particular had difficulty putting events in perspective. Their order had been racked by an intense internal quarrel which was adjudicated in 1517, although the wounds certainly were not healed by that settlement. In South Germany, the Mariological controversy between the Franciscans and Dominicans had boiled over so that princes and city councils had seen fit to intervene in an attempt to restore order and integrity. Were they now to believe that the rumblings of controversy in Saxony signaled the beginning of an upheaval which would outstrip all of these previous conflicts?

This period of confusion and uncertainty lasted about five years after Luther posted his theses. The widespread hesitance in South Germany to condemn his position decisively was due in part to the sympathetic response to Luther's attack on abuses. For example, the dukes of Bavaria, as well as the City Council of Nuremberg, had restricted the sale of indulgences in their jurisdictions before Luther's attack had made the issue so famous.[1]

Luther's challenge was not acknowledged as the one and only burning issue of the moment. Instead, this new threat was woven into the existing fabric of political and religious conflicts. For the dukes of Bavaria, the Lutheran question was a further complication of their relation to the emperor and to the powerful imperial cities of Bavaria. The dukes sought to extract from the papacy promises of increased control over the Bavarian Church, together with a prosperous ecclesiastical office for their younger brother, in return for their adoption of a hard line against Lutheranism. Hence, it was not until the years 1523/1524 that Bavarian officials began to suppress Lutheranism effectively.[2]

In the great cities the first reaction was to temporize. When John Eck appeared in Augsburg in 1520 with *Exsurge domine* in hand, prompt compliance was not forthcoming. In order to have the bull published and enforced, he needed the support of the City Council as well as that of the bishop. Since Eck could not obtain the consent of all parties to have the bull enforced immediately, Lutheran writings continued to circulate in the city.[3]

In Nuremberg, too, the City Council was caught between conflicting pressures. The Council was approving the appointments of preachers who openly advocated the Reformation even though John Eck in particular was pressing for the suppression of Lutherans. Eck had added to the list of those excommunicated as Lutherans the names of Lazarus Spengler and Willibald Pirckheimer, both prominent in the political and intellectual affairs of the city. Even though the edict of Worms had been posted in the town hall, Lutheran preaching was heard and Luther's writings were available.[4] Likewise in Basel, the City Council resisted papal attempts of 1520 to prohibit the distribution of Luther's writings.[5]

Thus for the first years decisive actions were not taken and decisive lines were not drawn. Within the Franciscan order a similar confusion persisted. Luther was not immediately identified as a threat to the existence of the order.

LUTHER AMONG THE FRANCISCANS

The Basel friary under the intellectual leadership of Pellican proved to be most fruitful ground for the reception of Luther's writings. Pellican in his chronicle recounted his first impressions upon seeing the ninety-five theses. He recalled his surprise over Luther's retention of the concept of purgatory. Pellican claimed

---

[33] For a sociological analysis of St. Francis's career see Heribert Roggen, "Die Lebensform des hl. Franziskus in ihrem Verhältnis zur Gesellschaft Italiens," *FS* **46** (1964): pp. 2–57, 287–321.

[1] Gerald Strauss, "The Religious Policies of Dukes Wilhelm and Ludwig of Bavaria in the First Decade of the Protestant Era," *Church History*, **28** (1959): p. 353. *Cf.* Reicke, *op. cit.*, pp. 690–692.

[2] Strauss, "The Religious Policies . . . ," pp. 352–362.
[3] Friedrich Zoepfl, *Geschichte des Bistums Augsburgs und seiner Bischöfe* (2 v., Munich, 1955–1969) **2**: pp. 18–25. *Cf.* Bauerreiss, *op. cit.* **6**: pp. 20–27 and Wolfgang Zorn, *Augsburg, Geschichte einer deutschen Stadt* (Munich, 1955), pp. 169–172.
[4] Strauss, *Nuremberg*, pp. 162–164. *Cf.* Gerhard Pfeiffer, "Entscheidung zur Reformation" in *Nürnberg-Geschichte einer europäischen Stadt* (Munich, 1971), pp. 146–148.
[5] Wackernagel, *Geschichte*, **3**: p. 323.

that he had called the whole idea into question as a result of his patristic researches. For the rest, he found Luther to be a proponent of that kind of doctrinal reform to which he had devoted several decades of activity. Very quickly, Basel became an important center for the publication of Luther's writings. Pellican was called upon to assist in preparing the Reformer's writings for the press.[6]

Pellican's atempt to minimize the radicality of Luther might be dismissed as a reflection of the envy of Swiss Reformers toward Luther. But Pellican was not one who promoted petty divisiveness. Two decades of research had prepared him to comment insightfully on Luther's theses. Further, Pellican's outlook was broadly ecumenical. He exchanged friendly correspondence with Luther although he later joined Zwingli in Zurich. But his essential vision was not limited to the encouragement of a united Protestantism. He insisted that there was no cause for a rupture in Christendom. The reform of doctrine, he insisted, was not a sign of his disobedience but instead a fulfillment of his duty. He granted Luther a place in this continuing tradition of reform. For his own part, Pellican saw no conflict between reading Luther's writings and continuing in the friary.[7]

In March, 1520, Pellican wrote to Luther expressing his admiration for the Reformer's achievements and expressing concern about the direction events were taking. After informing Luther about the rapid progress his writings were making through the presses of Basel and the eager reception they found in the city, Pellican went on to express his concern that excesses might result from the critical mood Luther had created. Pellican was cautious not to blame Luther directly for any excesses. He did, however, report that the respected Franciscan leader, Schatzgeyer, had expressed the view that John Eck had been more temperate than Luther in their exchange. Even though Pellican himself could tolerate the Scotists who dominated his order, he granted that Luther needed to use a sharp pen in order to get his critical point across.

It was not Luther but some of his circle whom Pellican feared. Some critics, "Erasmians" he called them, might lead others astray with their excesses. They could be irresponsible and divisive, they could be interpreted as admonishing others to throw off all restraint. In particular Pellican felt that a total condemnation of religious orders was not appropriate.

But surely the tone of the letter was not to rebuke Luther. In his praise of Luther, Pellican repeated his admiration for the Reformer's erudition. Many scholastic theologians were green with envy at Luther's success, he reported, but they were afraid to challenge him because of his great learning. To Pellican, Luther's achievement was, above all else, a triumph of learning.[8]

Pellican's enthusiasm for the new movement was shared by some of his colleagues. John Lüthard emerged in 1520 as the most prominent popular preacher of Reformation persuasion in Basel. Lüthard delivered a series of exegetical sermons on the gospels with materials drawn heavily from commentaries by the early fathers. His preaching attracted a great following and thereby further identified the Basel friary with the cause of Lutheranism. The friary church was used as a meeting place for assemblies of the local populace supporting the Reformation in 1522.

Pellican pictured Basel as a city alive with interest in the controversial pamphlets and sermons of the Reformers. He thought that a policy of suppression of these writings aimed at assuring that only trained theologians might deal with the issues under debate was neither possible nor advisable. The very success of the printing industry made confiscation of copies so difficult. Further Pellican considered the public airing of the theological questions among the laity to be a healthy ventilation of a theology in the grip of the "Scotists," whom he so fervently disliked.[9]

Scattered reports of other followers of Luther came from various friaries in South Germany but no other house was so definitively on the Reformers' side. In Ulm, John Eberlin of Günzburg, *lector* from 1519 to 1521, was attracted to Luther's writings. A powerful and controversial personality, Eberlin was so vehement in his espousal of the Reformation cause that he aroused great enmity among his colleagues. In spite of his popularity with the people of Ulm, Eberlin was forced to leave the friary and start out on a journey that was to lead him to Wittenberg and to a career of composing harsh attacks on monastic life.[10] Likewise from Ingolstadt came the report that the guardian of the friary there was accused in 1522 of being "Lutheran" because he supported the reception of the Eucharist in two kinds by the laity.[11]

But the supporters of Luther were in the minority. The great majority of the friars in South Germany eventually came to resist the new currents. In Nuremberg the Franciscan House heard the Lutheran teachings espoused by Augustinian friars and after 1521 echoed in the preaching of Andreas Osiander. Luther's

---

[6] Pellican, *Chronikon*, pp. 67, 75.

[7] See the author's, "Caspar Schatzgeyer and Conrad Pellican . . . ," pp. 191–193, 197, 198. *Cf.* Kurt Maeder, *Die Via Media in der Schweizerischen Reformation,* in: Zürcher Beiträge zur Reformationsgeschichte 2 (Zurich, 1970): pp. 134–142.

[8] Pellican to Luther *WA Br* 2: pp. 64–70.

[9] Pellican, *Chronikon,* pp. 75–86. Pellican's cautious approval of Luther resembles early comments made by Oecolampadius. See *Oecolampadii iudicium de doctore Martino Luthero* (Leipzig, 1520). For the later development of Pellican's attitudes toward toleration and the citation of his work by Sebastian Castellio see Roland H. Bainton, ed., *Concerning Heretics . . . an anonymous work attributed to Sebastian Castellio* (2nd ed., New York, 1965).

[10] Bernhard Riggenbach, *John Eberlin von Günzburg und sein Reformprogramm* (2nd ed., Nieuwkoop, 1967), pp. 12–19; hereafter cited as Riggenbach, *Eberlin.*

[11] Vitus Anton Winter, *Geschichte der Schicksale der evangelische Lehre in und durch Baiern* (Munich, 1809) 1: p. 84.

teachings were warmly received and commended by the *Sodalitas Staupitziana,* a fellowship of prominent citizens who gathered in the Augustinian friary to discuss the themes John Staupitz had dwelt on during his frequent visits to the city. In 1517 Wenceslas Linck came from the Augustinian house in Wittenburg to be preacher to the Augustinians in Nuremberg. Soon the admirers of Staupitz were becoming followers of Luther. The City Council became all the more determined to forbid the local sale of indulgences.[12]

From 1517 to 1520 the influential Schatzgeyer, former provincial, was guardian of the Nuremberg friary. Thus it was in the Nuremberg of Linck and Osiander that Schatzgeyer first began to shape his reaction to the new teachings. Schatzgeyer's first instinct was to mediate the dispute. Speaking in 1525 with the wisdom of hindsight, Schatzgeyer conceded that he had not immediately grasped the significance of Luther's attacks. He had at first taken Luther's writings to be a legitimate representation of Christian doctrine and spirit. Only after he had concluded that Luther's followers were bent on the destruction of a millennium of ecclesiastical growth did Schatzgeyer launch a counter attack. As late as 1522, even after the vigorous preaching of Linck and Osiander, Schatzgeyer published a conciliatory review of the doctrinal dispute. With this essay he sought to calm the troubled waters. His *Scrutinium Divinae Scripturae* is a monument to the years of confusion.

The work was prefaced by a commendation by Pellican. Pellican, who likewise deplored the division into two camps, presented the document as a search for compromise, a *via media.* Further, Pellican sought to ingratiate Schatzgeyer with humanist circles. He commented that even though Schatzgeyer was old in years, he was young in his zeal in the pursuit of languages.[13]

Although Pellican described the work as an attempt to compromise the issues involved, the *Scrutinium* could more accurately be called a restrained restatement of traditional scholastic teaching. First of all Schatzgeyer made it clear that he was not as enamored with humanist learning as Pellican suggested. Schatzgeyer remarked that much of the conflict in theological circles was the result of the introduction of foreign disciplines such as logic and science into the theological sphere. Further, Schatzgeyer expressed his skepticism regarding the zealous pursuit of Greek and Hebrew in addition to Latin. According to Schatzgeyer's admonitions, erudition was to be permitted only if it was very carefully harnessed to Christian piety.[14]

The title of the work suggested a concession to the call for a scriptural theology. As a matter of fact, Schatzgeyer made it abundantly clear that he considered the scholastic theologians to be standing in unbroken continuity with the early fathers and the scriptures. Although he quoted primarily from scripture he paused at one point to emphasize his view of the consonance of scripture with later church traditions. After reviewing the debate regarding the relationship of grace and free will and after defending the notion that man must "do what is in him" he concluded that this teaching was supported by scripture as well as by the authority of Thomas, Bonaventura, Alexander of Hales, and Scotus.

The document was more important for its tone than for its content. Repeatedly Schatzgeyer deplored the violence, the war, the tumult. According to his line of argument no substantive issues were at stake. The conflict was a war of words. In one passage he suggested that this debate was simply a continuation of the unfortunate divisiveness that had long existed among scholastic theologians. Some theologians, he said, call themselves Thomists, other Scotists. Some say they learned from Augustine, others from Jerome.[15] It was not so much the teaching of theologians as their behavior which he deplored. Whereas Pellican advocated the return to primitive sources in the original tongue, Schatzgeyer urged theologians to seek the unity of love.

The conciliatory tone of the *Scrutinium* can best be illustrated by referring to Schatzgeyer's comments on the debate over the doctrine of justification. Schatzgeyer acknowledged that diversity of opinion existed regarding the severity of the impact of sin on the spiritual potency of man. Some had taught that the first sin had deprived man of certain praeter-human spiritual endowments given to man before the fall. The other, more pessimistic view, asserted that in addition to losing these praeter-human endowments man's nature itself had been severely wounded by sin.

These differing views posited contradictory theological anthropologies. Proponents of the first view held out hope that man could take the first step on the road toward justification. By contrast, those who had insisted that man's nature was seriously wounded could insist quite logically on the primacy of grace.

At this point in the debate, Schatzgeyer made his mediating suggestion. The root issue of the debate, he observed, was the charge that the first view was "Pelagian." But was this charge justified?

Schatzgeyer adduced the nominalist doctrine of God as a defense of the orthodoxy of the first view. Let us grant, Schatzgeyer said, that man takes the first step and that God responds with the gift of grace. The divine response is not a reward earned by man. Quite the contrary, God acts out of his unlimited generosity in responding to man's feeble effort. Thus Schatzgeyer concluded that both positions were within the pale

---

[12] Höss, *op. cit.,* pp. 145, 146. *Cf.* David Curtis Steinmetz, *Misericordia Dei, The Theology of Johannes von Staupitz in its Late Medieval Setting* (Leiden, 1968).

[13] *Scrutinium divinae scripturae pro conciliatione dissidentium dogmatum,* edited by Ulrich Schmidt, in: Corpus Catholicorum 5 (Münster/W., 1922): pp. 1, 2; hereafter cited as *Scrutinium.*
[14] *Ibid.,* pp. 24, 25.

[15] *Ibid.,* pp. 7, 21–23.

of orthodoxy.[16] By lmplication Schatzgeyer suggested that the theological debate on this point should continue with neither side attempting to read the other out of the Church.

Further, Schatzgeyer suggested that the Reformers' call for a teaching of justification by faith alone could be accommodated within the realm of more traditional scholastic theology. Schatzgeyer pointed out quite correctly that nominalistic theology had taught a baptismal justification by faith alone. So he concluded, the Reformers could have their justification by faith alone in the form of this baptismal justification but they in turn must accept the concept of a justification by works in the adult life.[17]

Thus did Schatzgeyer patiently recite old answers to sharp new questions. Let the debate continue, he argued, without divisiveness and rancor. Schatzgeyer saw the beginnings of the Reformation as still another quarrel among scholastic theologians. If his brethren would only watch their tempers, if they would only search for points of agreement instead of emphasizing disagreement, the basic unity of Christian truth would soon emerge. Reconciliation and not heresy hunting was the order of the day.

MURNER'S REACTION

Thomas Murner waited until 1520 before committing himself to print on the question of Luther's writings. He published a comparatively mild admonition to Luther counseling him to keep his silence until the issues were determined. This admonition was accompanied by a critical commentary on Luther's writings. It must be said on behalf of Murner that by 1520 he had grasped the significance of the debate. Although he chose a tone of brotherly warning in his letter to Luther, he had no inclination to underestimate the nature of the conflict.

First there was a marked legal tone to Murner's approach to the question. He took note of Luther's appeal to a future council but he contended that this did not provide grounds for continued exposition of a point of view which had been condemned by the church hierarchy. Specifically, he urged Luther not to preach without ecclesiastical approval. In his comment to the public on Luther's writings, he suggested that the appeal to the Council was really a stalling tactic. Luther, he observed, was not willing to submit to any judge on earth.[18] In the same pamphlets Murner harshly criticized Luther's popular appeal. The simple people, he suggested, were being confused by the complicated issues of theology. He saw Luther's use of vernacular language in his writings as a demagogic tactic designed to take the issues out of the professional theological context where they belonged and place them instead before the unlearned populace. Theology, he insisted, was for those properly trained, not for the common man.[19]

Further, Murner warned of the results which might come were a revolution set loose. He granted that there were evils in the Church which needed to be reformed carefully. But he feared that Luther was spurring on rebels to destroy much more than the evils alone. Murner pointed to the example of Bohemia where priests were murdered and the churches leveled. He issued to Luther the prophetic warning that he should be careful lest he achieve far more than he ever intended.[20]

Finally, Murner gave Luther instructions on certain theological points which Murner was totally unwilling to sacrifice. He defended the validity of ecclesiastical tradition alongside scripture. Using Biblical quotations, he supported the contention that the mass was a real sacrifice, not merely a testament. He upheld the visible, hierarchical Church against Luther's criticism, which he put down as an echo of teachings promulgated by Hus and Wycliffe.[21]

CONCLUSION

Decisions about the future of the new movement were to be made by many parties—city councils and princes, humanists and publishers, theologians and bishops. At first neither the direction nor the impact of the decisions was clear. Countervailing forces neutralized each other. Many sought to temporize.

The Franciscans contributed to the early confusion. They did not immediately comprehend that the Reformation would threaten the very existence of their order. Only after reformed cities began to close down friaries did the Franciscans become the spearheads of the Counter Reformation.[22]

VI. POLICIES AND THEOLOGIES

The popular support of the Reformation forced crises in city after city in South Germany bringing to an end the city councils' time of temporizing. In some cases, the crisis arose when popular sentiment opposed disciplinary steps taken by the ecclesiastical hierarchy against supporters of the Reformation. In other cities the dissonance between the versions of the Christian message preached from different pulpits finally became too harsh to bear. Whatever the specific incitement, the city councils began, in the early 1520's, to take a firm position in regard to the Reformation dispute.

By resolving the Reformation dispute, the city councils usurped ecclesiastical prerogatives. Intervention

---

[16] *Ibid.*, pp. 16–20. For literature on the background of this problem see Heiko Augustinus Oberman, *The Harvest of Medieval Theology* (Cambridge, Mass., 1963).

[17] *Scrutinium*, pp. 38–45. For the nominalist discussion of baptism see Oberman, *op. cit.*, pp. 134, 135.

[18] "Ein christliche und briederliche ermanung," pp. 31–37 and "Von Doctor Martinus luters leren und predigen," pp. 94–96 both cited from *Thomas Murners Deutsche Schriften* (Berlin, 1927) **6**, edited by Wolfgang Pfeiffer-Belli.

[19] "Von Doctor Martinus . . . ," pp. 91, 92. *Cf.* "Ein christliche . . . ," p. 31.

[20] "Ein christliche . . . ," pp. 40, 41, 83, 84.

[21] *Ibid.*, pp. 48–50, 78.

[22] *Cf.* Bauerreiss, *op. cit.*, **6**: pp. 69, 70.

by the councils on behalf of Reformers threatened by ecclesiastical disciplinary action signaled the demise of hierarchical discipline over the clergy in these cities.

In an attempt to harmonize the dissident views heard from the many pulpits of the town, some city councils called for open theological discussions or disputations. Further, the councils themselves chose the arbiters who presided and determined the orthodox message to be propagated in the city. In these instances, the church effectively lost the authority to judge the orthodoxy of preaching.

As city councils made definitive declarations for the Reformation, they proceeded immediately to disestablish the religious houses within the town. The friaries with their power to hear confession and read anniversary masses were the symbols of the old order which the Reformation would no longer tolerate. With unfailing precision, the city councils moved from a declaration for the Reformation to the establishment of a procedure for destroying the vitality of the friaries.

NUREMBERG

The pressure to take a definitive stand weighed heavily on the City Council of Nuremberg. John Eck had made a special point of singling out prominent citizens of Nuremberg as subjects of excommunication in the same bull which banned Luther in 1520. Further, the Diet of Worms had decided that future meetings of the Estates should take place there. Thus the city was in the spotlight at a moment when imperial policy held that Luther's teachings were to be suppressed.[1]

The insurgents were led by Andreas Osiander, who emerged from the Augustinian friary where he had been a teacher of Hebrew, to take the post of preacher at St. Lorenz. From 1522 on, Osiander led a chorus of young preachers who rapidly attracted large segments of the population to the Lutheran cause. Even though the pressure on the Council increased, it still sought temporary, pragmatic solutions. Thus when the Franciscan preacher, John Wintzler, came to the attention of the Council in 1522, the Council's stated concern was to avoid clamor. The Franciscan House, where Wintzler preached so vigorously against Luther, together with the Dominican House, was known as a defender of the old order. After consulting with Osiander, the Council found Wintzler guilty, not of preaching against Lutheranism but rather of creating uproar within the city. They forced him to leave Nuremberg.[2]

The expulsion of one preacher did not silence the Franciscans. In March, 1524, a new Franciscan preacher, Jeremias Mulich, was called before the Council. Again the Council objected not so much to the specific doctrines he preached—original and actual sin, penance, and miracles are mentioned—as to the fact that his preachings aroused extreme disfavor among inhabitants of the town. The guardian of the Franciscan House was asked to prohibit any further preaching by Mulich, a decision which the guardian received with considerable displeasure. The friars attempted to appeal their case to the Council with a statement of their theological positions. This the Council turned down very curtly noting that their concern was to maintain the peace, not to have a learned disputation. Such a disputation the Council noted, Mulich could have with "gelert leut," a designation the Council clearly did not apply to itself.[3]

In spite of papal and imperial opinion, the city was moving rapidly to the Lutheran side. In 1524 the definitive confrontation between the ecclesiastical hierarchy and the City Council took place. The bishop of Bamberg decided to move judicially against Reformation preachers in Nuremberg. The priors of St. Sebalt and St. Lorenz together with Wolfgang Volprecht, prior of the Augustinians, all known for their Lutheran persuasions, were brought to the episcopal court and charged with serving the Eucharist in both kinds. The Lutheran preachers protested the judicial action and declared that even though they were to be obedient to their bishop, such obligations could not lead them to act contrary to the Biblical mandate. They appealed to the decision of a future council. The episcopal court found them guilty of the charges and was prepared to carry out a sentence of suspension from office and excommunication. However, at this point the City Council, acting upon the recommendation of Lazarus Spengler, intervened in defense of the accused. Spengler pointed out that given the Reformation sympathies of the town, this episcopal action was unlikely to dissuade the followers of these preachers from their Lutheran convictions. Spengler encouraged the Council to break new ground and take jurisdiction in the case. This it did by sheltering the preachers from episcopal authority and permitting them to continue in their positions.[4]

As a result of this controversy, the two priors of the town parishes published a defense of their conduct of the mass addressed to the bishop of Bamberg. They made a special point of attacking anniversary masses, the clerical service so frequently associated with the

---

[1] Strauss, *Nuremberg*, pp. 162, 163.

[2] Gottfried Seebass, *Das reformatorische Werk des Andreas Osiander* (Nuremberg, 1967), pp. 91, 92. *Cf.* Mauritius Demuth, "Johannes Winzler, ein Franziskaner aus der Reformationszeit," *FS* 4 (1917): pp. 257–261.

[3] SAN, Ratsbuch 12; 227, 227v, 228, 235. *Cf.* Gerhard Pfeiffer, "Die Einführung der Reformation in Nürnberg als kirchenrechtliches und bekenntniskundliches Problem," *Blätter für deutsche Landesgeschichte* 89 (1952): pp. 114, 115. See also Pfeiffer's "Entscheidung zur Reformation," in *Nürnberg-Geschichte einer europäischen Stadt* (Munich, 1971), pp. 146–154.

[4] Pfeiffer, "Die Einführung . . . ," pp. 116–122. For a comment on the decisive role of the Council in the early stages of the Reformation in Nuremberg see Gottfried Seebass, "Die Reformation in Nürnberg," *Mitteilungen des Vereins für Geschichte der Stadt Nürnberg* 55 (1967/1968): pp. 259–264. A revised version of this article is published in translation in *The Social History of the Reformation*, edited by Lawrence P. Buck and Jonathon W. Zophy (Columbus, 1972), pp. 17–40.

friary. Anniversary masses which had to be purchased amounted to financial discrimination in religious matters, they argued. Though the Church could raise money by celebrating such masses, the poor were left without equal spiritual advantage. In fact, they continued, the spiritual benefits of masses could go only to the living. Therefore, they concluded, anniversary masses should be eliminated not merely because they were a financial scandal but more importantly, because they rested on insecure theological foundations.[5]

The Council confirmed its control over ecclesiastical affairs by intervening in a dispute which arose in the Carthusian House. Blasius Stöckl had been accused by other brothers in the house of heretical preaching. The house had found the charges justified and sent him to another house as a form of discipline. This action the Council found intolerable. The Council declared that Stöckl should be permitted to remain and that those who had made the charges against him should be expelled. Further, an Augustinian was assigned to preach in the house in hopes that he might soften the recalcitrance there.[6]

By these actions, the Council demonstrated that it would contravene ecclesiastical discipline in order to protect the Reformation. In addition, it was now clear that *ad hoc* actions on specific cases would no longer suffice. Therefore the Council moved to establish a new norm of orthodoxy for Nuremberg. Having concluded that the town could no longer tolerate the clash of dissident theologies, the Council declared that all of the town's preachers should draw up written statements of their theology and discuss them together in hopes that common ground might be found.

The opposition to the Lutherans was led by the preachers of the Franciscan, Dominican, and Carmelite houses. They objected repeatedly to the ground rules which the Council established. First, they noted that religious disputations were forbidden by imperial mandate. To this the Council replied that a friendly discussion, not a disputation, was envisioned. Further, they insisted that, if a theological discussion were to be held, the final determination of right and wrong should be made by the theological faculties of the Universities of Heidelberg, Ingolstadt, and Tübingen. This objection pinpointed quite precisely the "revolution" occurring in the city. The Council would not accept the late medieval norms for determining orthodox teaching within the Church. The religious affairs of Nuremberg were to be settled within the city by means chosen by the City Council.

The worst fears of the Council's opponents were fulfilled. A hostile crowd greeted them when they arrived for the disputation. Osiander swayed the assembly with his powerful statement of the Reformation position. Before the disputation had concluded, the dissident friars protested the nature of the proceedings and refused to participate further. When the Council could not achieve a voluntary consensus it ordered the establishment of a new orthodoxy. The proponents of the old teaching were ordered to cease preaching and hearing confession until their position had become "Biblical." Those preachers who had attacked the Council proceedings were expelled from the town.[7]

The friaries, those symbols of the old order, found their active days at an end. In late 1524 the Augustinians and Dominicans had anticipated the outcome and arranged for the closing of their houses. After the disputation of March, 1525, the Franciscans were ordered to preach in the friary church only upon occasions when no lay people were present. Further, they were forbidden to accept any new members into the house. No longer was an active Franciscan house to be a part of Nuremberg life.

BASEL

The Basel friary was not the target of the insurgent preachers. To the contrary, the friary was a rallying point for those who adhered to the new message. With Pellican as guardian and Lüthard as preacher, the Franciscans became known for their receptiveness to Luther's teachings.

As was true in the other cities the ecclesiastical hierarchy moved to stem the tide of popularity which the Reformation preachers were enjoying. In 1522 an episcopal mandate concerning preaching was issued. The mandate forbade any further attacks on ecclesiastical institutions and laws. All who preached were to interpret the gospel as it had been traditionally interpreted by the Church. In sum, the mandate plainly called for the preachers of the new message to cease their activity.[8]

Nor was the Franciscan order unconcerned about the rise of "Lutheranism" within its ranks. The General Chapter meeting at Capri in 1521 made it incumbent upon all friars to work for the extirpation of this "Lutheranism" which was inimical to human salvation. In addition, Caspar Schatzgeyer was named in 1523 as inquisitor for South German Franciscans.[9]

In 1523 pressures against the continuing Reformation activity in the Basel friary mounted to the point that Schatzgeyer, the provincial, was forced to take action. Both the cathedral clergy in the city and theologians at the university had complained about the activities of the Franciscans. Although he was accompanied by John Wintzler, the hard line opponent of the new teaching in Nuremberg, Schatzgeyer was deter-

---

[5] *Grundt und Ursach aus der heiligen schrifft wie und warumb die eer wirdigen Herren baider Pfarrkirchen . . . die Misspreuch bey der heyligen Mess . . . abgestelt, undterlassen und geendert haben* (Nuremberg, 1525).

[6] Adolf Engelhardt, "Die Reformation in Nürnberg," *Mitteilungen des Vereins für Geschichte der Stadt Nürnberg* 33 (1936): pp. 163–165.

[7] *Ibid.*, pp. 167–181.

[8] *Aktensammlung zur Geschichte der Basler Reformation in den Jahren 1519 bis Anfang 1534*, edited by Emil Dürr and Paul Roth (6 v., Basel, 1921–1950) 1: pp. 38–40.

[9] *AM* 16: p. 140 and Nikolaus Paulus, *op. cit.*, p. 61.

mined to work out an amicable solution. He proposed that Pellican, his friend and former associate, be transferred without prejudice to the position of guardian in Kaysersberg. Although Lüthard was to be replaced by Wintzler as friary preacher, Schatzgeyer was willing to accept Lüthard as his assistant and traveling companion.[10] Had Schatzgeyer's decisions been permitted, the objectionable friars would have been removed from Basel but under honorable circumstances.

As was the case in Nuremberg, the City Council intervened at this point, unwilling to allow the proposed disciplinary action against advocates of the new preaching. Two representatives of the Council were sent to Schatzgeyer asking that he present a written statement of charges against the friars. This Schatzgeyer refused to do, so the Council informed him that if the proposed action were taken all the Franciscans would be expelled from the town. Schatzgeyer requested and was given a personal audience before the Council to discuss this action. The record of the Council's forthright decision to intervene in this matter of ecclesiastical discipline is one of the most crucial documents marking the beginning of the Reformation in Basel.

The Council reported that Schatzgeyer made some statement defending the right of preachers to be less than fully candid in dealing with laity (*gmein man*). The Council further made clear that this point was not gladly received. Confirming Pellican's estimate of the lay attitude in Basel, the city fathers declared that the laity would take decisive action to protect the friars. Schatzgeyer was told to keep hands off. In addition, the Council ordered that the two university theologians who had launched the charges against the friary should be removed from their positions and that Pellican and Oecolampadius should be installed in their places.[11]

The City Council had now declared, in effect, that it would nulify ecclesiastical jurisdiction if such became necessary. But as was the case in Nuremberg, if the Council was to deny to the ecclesiastical hierarchy the authority to settle the theological disputes, then the Council itself was forced to become theological arbiter. Shortly after the Franciscan decision was rendered, the Council issued its own mandate governing preaching in Basel. The mandate was more pragmatic than theological. The city fathers declared that they were concerned with the confusion generated by preachers who contradicted one another from the pulpit. They lamented the lot of the faithful who earnestly wished to follow Christian teaching but did not know which road to take. It was decreed that preaching should be "evangelical." The message of the preaching was not to be that of Luther or any other doctor but simply that of the gospel. Although the mandate begged the essential questions under debate, none of the disputants could criticize the stand which had been taken.[12]

Pellican also searched for some basis of compromise between the Basel friary and the leaders of the South German Province. Shortly after Schatzgeyer had been sent packing by the Council, Pellican composed a long letter to the provincial capital in Landshut. Far from crowing over his victory, Pellican made clear that the conflict had pained him just as it had Schatzgeyer. The letter contained no discussions of putting off the habit or leaving the friary. Pellican desired some sort of reconciliation which would keep the Basel house in good standing with the rest of the province.[13]

First, Pellican addressed himself to the question of the proper theological reaction to Luther's teachings. He reported that the popular reception of Luther's writings in Basel was such that they could not be ignored. The faithful were reading Luther's writings and asking for guidance in reacting to them. Hence, Pellican suggested that it was the duty of the clergy to read Luther's writings in order to respond intelligently. Pellican himself had read Luther's writings but was not willing to issue any blanket judgment regarding them. He agreed with many of the points made by Luther but disagreed vehemently with others.

In addition, Pellican made it clear that in his view Luther's teachings had not, as yet, received a fair trial. He described both the standards by which he thought Luther's teachings should be judged and the kind of body which should make the determination. The first standard for judgment should be conformity with the teaching of Christ and the Apostles and the traditions and usages of the primitive church. Beyond that the fathers and the later teachings of the church should serve as a standard to the extent that such traditions were unequivocal and in accordance with Scripture. As to the jury, it should consist of men who were pious, learned, and faithful but, most of all, not caught up in the entanglements of this world. Neither the court of the emperor nor the chambers of city councils contained the men who met Pellican's standards. Still Pellican had to admit that he had made tentative judgments regarding this question. In his view, Luther came much closer to presenting an evangelical position than did the scholastics whose writings had become so dependent on philosophy.

Finally, Pellican had a practical proposal aimed at maintaining peace within the various friaries of the province. He suggested that any friar who was dissatisfied in Basel should be free to transfer to a house he found more congenial. Further, friars from through-

---

[10] Bernhard Riggenbach, "Die Barfüsserkirche als Geburtsstätte der Reformation," in *Festbuch zur Eröffnung des historischen Museums* (Basel, 1894), pp. 111–113. *Cf.* Demuth, *op. cit.*, p. 261.

[11] The Council deliberations as reported in the Ratsbuch are available in Dürr, *op. cit.* 1: pp. 61–63.

[12] Dürr, *op. cit.* 1: pp. 65–69. The eventual adoption of a protestant orthodoxy by the Basel City Council in 1529 is described by Paul Roth, *Durchbruch and Festsetzung der Reformation in Basel*, in: Basler Beiträge zur Geschichtswissenschaft 8 (Basel, 1942).

[13] The text of the letter is found in Pellican's *Chronikon*, pp. 83–95.

out the province who supported Luther's teachings should be permitted to take up residence in Basel.

Pellican's desire to reconcile opposing forces was not to be granted. Although he continued to reside in Basel for the next two years, his life was full of conflict. The Provincial Chapter meeting in 1523 did not grant Pellican's wish for compromise but instead assigned a new guardian to the Basel friary who took office with an intent to restore orthodoxy there. Even though the personal impropriety of this guardian caused him to be replaced, the tensions within the friary continued. Acting out of fear that the friary food might be poisoned, Adam Petri had an outside food supply sent in to Pellican.[14]

Before his departure in 1526 to join Zwingli in Zurich, Pellican together with Lüthard continued a strange mixture of new teaching and old ways. They both continued to wear the friar's habit and Lüthard officiated at mass while continuing his evangelical preaching.[15]

Not only the conservatives within his own order, but Erasmus as well, took Pellican to task for his position. The occasion for the dispute with Erasmus was the publication in 1525 by Oecolampadius of a treatise on the nature of Christ's presence in the Eucharist. The Basel City Council, confronted with the necessity of making a determination regarding this writing, had written to Erasmus for his opinion. Erasmus had replied that it strayed too far from the teaching of the Church. But then Erasmus heard rumors that Pellican was claiming Erasmian support for Oecolampadius.

Erasmus wrote to chastise Pellican. The prince of the humanists insisted that he would never accept a merely symbolic view of the Eucharist. He feared that such views led to thoroughly unwanted implications. The Reformation had opened a Pandora's box which could not be shut. Luther had already gone too far in breaking with traditional teachings of the Church. If one began going down that road by agreeing with Luther, Erasmus contended, then one would soon find himself further down the road agreeing with Carlstadt.[16]

In reply, Pellican used those arguments which had been so common to Christian humanism before the outbreak of the Reformation. What was included in the traditional consensus of the church, he asked. Surely it did not include everything that came from the pen of any active religious writer. The humanists themselves had uncovered the spurious writings and questioned the authority of statements issued by ecclesiastical councils of dubious authenticity.

Further, Pellican was unwilling to put the question in terms of becoming committed to a Luther or a Carlstadt. He would retain his own integrity as a theologian and measure those men against the consensus of the Church as he understood it and as that consensus might be newly interpreted by a council acting on evangelical principles. In sum, Pellican refused to accept Erasmus's judgment that he had excommunicated himself from the consensus of the Church by associating with radical theologians.[17]

By 1525 Pellican had also come to despair of any reconciliation with the leaders of the South German Province. He wrote a defiant letter totally different in tone from his attempt at compromise of two years earlier. He complained of the harassment from which he suffered in the friary and pointed out that were he to move elsewhere, as some had suggested, the harassment would only be worse. Denying that he had abandoned the ideals of the order, Pellican insisted that he now followed those ideals more perfectly without depending on any special dispensations from the pope. The Observant movement had spoken of reforming the order. Their vision was too limited, Pellican said. All of Christendom needed to be reformed. He knew that the "papists" within the order would resist such a reform. However, the forces that had now been loosed would see that reform through to completion. As he closed his letter, Pellican made clear that he no longer anticipated a fair hearing for the "Lutherans." No one of that persuasion would even be permitted to speak before provincial authorities.[18]

This bitter letter was Pellican's valedictory to the Franciscan order. Early in 1526, he left for Zurich to become the Hebraist in Zwingli's theological circle. Shortly after arriving in Zurich, he married. Lüthard, who was much aggrieved at Zwingli's action in taking Pellican away from him, continued to be an active preacher of the Lutheran persuasion. Likewise, the friary church continued to be a meeting place for the adherents of the Reformation. It was, in fact, mass meetings in the Franciscan church in 1528 and 1529 which forced the City Council on to even more decisive steps in support of Reformation teachings.[19]

Pellican's break with the order was one of expediency, not of principle. In his Chronicle he spelled out carefully the events of his last years in Basel so that his descendants might know the truth regarding the reasons why he left the friary. He recorded this account to counter false rumors which had circulated regarding his reasons for leaving the order. In a letter written nearly a decade after Pellican left Basel, he made clear that he would not join with other former friars who sought to denigrate the disciplined religious life. In Pellican's view reformation teaching did not require the disavowal of the order. He abandoned an inflexible hierarchy, not the rule of St. Francis.[20]

---

[14] *Ibid.*, pp. 95–98.
[15] Willy Brändly, "Johannes Lüthard 'der Monch von Luzern,'" *Zwingliana* **8** (1946): pp. 315–317.
[16] Allen, *Ep.* **6**: pp. 209–211.
[17] *Ibid.*, pp. 216–219.
[18] Pellican, *Chronikon,* pp. 98–105.
[19] Riggenbach, "Die Barfüsserkirche als Geburtsstätte der Reformation," pp. 120, 121. Cf. Paul Roth, *op. cit.,* pp. 17, 18.
[20] Allen, *Ep.* **11**: p. 252.

STRASSBURG

In striking contrast to the friaries in Basel and Nuremberg, the Strassburg house, the seat of Conventual power in the South German Province, was not a flourishing brotherhood when the Reformation broke out. The decision not to adopt the Observant reform had robbed it of the vitality of that movement. Toward the end of the fifteenth century, a decline in numbers and financial strength was evident.[21] The early sixteenth century had been marked by bitter struggles in which Thomas Murner had played a prominent role. After his return to Strassburg in 1513 Murner had conducted a running battle with George Hoffman, the provincial of the Conventual wing.[22]

Weakened by these conflicts, the friary was in no position to make a stand for the old order. Thomas Murner alone stood out as a Franciscan defender of the status quo. When the dissolution of the friary was first broached to the Council in 1523, the new message had already made considerable progress in Strassburg. Matthäus Zell had begun his career of Reformation preaching. Wolfgang Capito, provost of the chapter of St. Thomas, followed Zell in declaring himself for the Reformation. Martin Bucer was present in Strassburg and would within several months be chosen by popular demand of the congregation as the preacher at St. Aurelie.[23]

The two friars who first appeared before the Council in November requested changes which amounted to the dissolution of the house. They reported having come to the realization that salvation came from faith and trust in God, not the habit and the seclusion of the friary. Therefore, they asked permission to put off the habit. They were prepared to turn over to the Council the financial affairs of the house, which they said were in a sad state of disarray. The friary school was the one function of the house they wished to continue in order to promote, "the common good and Christian love." Disillusioned with the religious vocation of their house, they wished to serve as school masters to Strassburg's children.[24]

The desire for such a change was not unanimous. No sooner had the proposal been made than George Hoffmann, the provincial resident in Strassburg, wrote to object that the statement had been made without his knowledge or approval. After investigating the matter, the Council concluded early in 1524 that the issue should be settled among the friars themselves. The Council added the admonition that the quarreling parties should act in the spirit of Christian charity.[25]

The Council could not dispose of the Franciscans so easily. The popular support for the new preachers was increasing as Bucer took up his post in February, 1524. A month later, a delegation of Franciscans was before the Council again, this time led by Murner. From the onset of the Reformation debate in Strassburg, Murner's controversial style had been a thorn in the side of the Council. In spite of Council censorship against controversial writings, Murner had insisted on publishing harsh attacks on the new teaching. The conflicts resulting from these publications had become so intense that Murner was transferred by his own Order to Augsburg in 1522. There, too, he wore out his welcome quickly but then was called to the court of Henry VIII in England in 1523 to help prepare a defense of traditional teaching. Upon his return to Strassburg, he found the friary on the verge of collapse.[26]

The statement Murner and his colleagues presented to the City Council conceded that the friary was near extinction but it blamed all the problems on Murner's long time enemy, George Hoffmann. The statement was, in fact, a long harangue claiming that Hoffmann was ruining the friary's reputation at the same time he was emptying its treasury. The Strassburg house, they claimed, was forced to bear the expenses of the overly elegant habits of the provincial. The table he set, they reported, was worthy of a prince. He rode through the city on a horse and even required that one of the friars serve as stable boy. He prohibited Strassburg friars from pursuing education only to berate them for their ignorance. Because of the evil reputation all friars bore from Hoffmann's behavior, Murner and his colleagues requested that they be permitted to give up the habit.[27]

The Council delayed no longer. Permission was given for members of the house to adopt lay clothes and to marry if they wished. An inventory was made of the property of the house and pensions were given to the former brothers. But Murner had not yet had enough of controversy. Forbidden by the Council to send additional attacks on the new preachers to the local publishers, he retaliated by setting up his own press in the friary. Further, he traveled to Nuremberg in 1524 where Cardinal Campeggio was present for the Imperial Diet. His criticisms of the town fathers to the cardinal were a considerable embarrassment to the Council. By September of that year, Murner found that he was no longer welcome in the city.[28] In 1525 the celebration of the mass in the friary was totally forbidden. The secularized friars who continued to live in the house left and the house was used as a school and then a poorhouse until it was torn down in 1529.[29]

The Franciscan house in Strassburg had not been a major source of agitation as the Reformation gained popularity in the town. The choice of preachers for the town parishes and their decisions to marry had forced the Council to contravene the actions of ecclesiastical

---

[21] See above, p. 10.
[22] Liebenau, *op. cit.*, pp. 79–84.
[23] Miriam Usher Chrisman, *Strabourg and the Reform* (New Haven, 1967), pp. 81–117.
[24] Eubel, *Geschichte*, pp. 72, 73. *Cf.* André Jung, *Beiträge zu der Geschichte der Reformation* (Strassburg and Leipzig, 1830), pp. 263, 264.
[25] Eubel, *Geschichte*, p. 73.
[26] Liebenau, *op. cit.*, pp. 169–200.
[27] Jung, *op. cit.*, pp. 264–267.
[28] *Ibid.*, pp. 267–271.
[29] Eubel, *Geschichte*, pp. 76, 77.

jurisdictions.³⁰ However, when the City Council took the decisive steps to defend Reformation preaching, the friaries, as symbols of the old order, came under attack. Because it was already weak, the Franciscan house succumbed quickly. There is little reason to suppose that a stronger house could have survived against the wave of popular support for Reformation preaching. In Strassburg also, the friaries were very quickly identified as symbols of the old order. Popular support for the Reformation, which several times took the form of threatening mobs, called for the dissolution of the symbols of the old order. In Strassburg too, the adoption of the Reformation meant not merely the acceptance of a new message, but the destructions of the strongholds of the old orthodoxy.³¹

OTHER CITIES

The friary in Augsburg produced an agitator far less sophisticated than his colleague in Basel. John Schilling, *lector* of the Franciscans, attacked the wealthy of Augsburg, especially the Fuggers, in the name of Luther. Since the first attempts were made to publish *Exsurge domine,* partisans and workers had rallied to the Lutheran banner. Schilling was reputed to have drunk wine with the weavers and to have advocated an equalitarian division of wealth. In August, 1524, the City Council expelled him. His followers, eighteen hundred strong, besieged the city hall. Slowly and grudgingly the Council gave ground until it agreed that Schilling might remain and that the mob would not be prosecuted. Schilling's cohorts frightened the city fathers. The Council was forced to protect itself with armed men. Jacob Fugger, fearing for the lives of prominent clergy, spirited them out of the city.

By 1526 the Franciscans were subject to a Council much more inclined to favor the Reformation. The guardian of the friary left to become a secular priest. He was replaced by a preacher of the Council's choosing, Michael Keller, noted as a Zwinglian. Nine years later the Council took definitive steps to make Augsburg a Protestant city. In that same year the last friars left the Franciscan house.³²

In other cities of the province where the Reformation was accepted, the friaries suffered a similar fate. In both Zurich and Bern, the official adoption of Protestantism included the drama of a city council-sponsored debate. Once the decision had been taken to opt for the Reformation, the friaries were among the first targets of the new leadership. Late in 1524, Zurich now firmly under Zwingli's control, ordered that all inhabitants of religious houses were not merely free to leave but that they now were required to become students or to learn a trade. Likewise in Bern, after the disputation of 1528, severe restrictions were put on the Franciscan house. All members were given permission to leave and marry. The house could accept no additional novices and any friar who chose to remain in the house could do so only if he lived according to the gospel.³³ In Frankfurt, the friars themselves offered their house to the City Council in 1529. Their leader, Peter Komberg, later became a Protestant preacher in the city. Only a minority of members in the house protested this dissolution.³⁴

The friary in Ulm was lost to the order after a decade of struggle. From 1519 to 1521 John Eberlin espoused Lutheran ideas in the friary. These years in Ulm marked the start of his violently pro-Lutheran and anti-Franciscan fulminations. After Eberlin's departure the friary became a stronghold of opposition to the new preaching. John Wintzler was present in 1525 and 1526 to defend traditional teachings. However, by the next year the Protestant tide was so strong that two recalcitrant Franciscan preachers were expelled from the city. Pressure from the City Council against the friary mounted until 1531 when the last inhabitants vacated the house.³⁵

Two decades after the eruption of the Reformation, the South German Province had been seriously weakened. About a half of the friaries were closed either in fact or in practice. Not only had the Province lost numbers, it lost strength. The friaries in Strassburg, Nuremberg, Basel, Augsburg, and Frankfurt had produced leaders for the province. Distinguished writers and preachers frequented these houses. In these cities the friars had conversed with famous humanists. The Reformation expelled the order from the great cultural centers of South Germany.³⁶

CONCLUSIONS

There was a shocking suddenness to the demise of the friaries in the great cities. Just a century earlier agreements for anniversary masses assumed that they would be continued in perpetuity. The friaries would surely exist until the end of the age. Even the Observant reform and the resulting rejection of anniversary masses seemed only to solidify the place of the friary in the city.

To be sure the friars were criticized but most often simply because they failed to meet their own high standards. The order clearly did not anticipate so stern a negative judgment. Glassberger's Chronicle ended on a triumphant note in the early sixteenth century. He witnessed the order marching victoriously to the new world. The possibility that his own house would be closed within two decades did not cross his mind.³⁷

---

³⁰ Chrisman, *op. cit.,* pp. 98–117.
³¹ For a discussion of popular agitation against religious houses in Strassburg, see Chrisman, pp. 138–154.
³² Friedrich Roth, *Augsburgs Reformationsgeschichte* (4 v., Munich, 1901) 1: pp. 156–169. *Cf.* Zorn, *op. cit.,* pp. 169–181.
³³ Eubel, *Geschichte,* pp. 78–81.
³⁴ Grän, "Frankfurt/Main," pp. 152–158.
³⁵ Johannes Gatz, "Ulm," *AFA* 2 (1958): pp. 20–34.
³⁶ For a review of friaries lost to the Reformation see Eubel, *Geschichte,* p. 68.
³⁷ Glassberger, pp. 524–526.

The friars fell victim to popular sentiment and political reaction. As a rule, city councils did not lead the way. They were pressured by broad popular support for the Reformation. The councils sought in vain to cope with the conflict by pragmatic, political measures, not ideological judgments.

Despite their intentions, the councils found themselves dragged willy nilly into decisions regarding the governance of the Church and eventually the judgment of doctrine. The choice of a preacher or the attempted discipline of a cleric could be so controversial that the Council was forced to guarantee an acceptable outcome. The next stage, Council participation in theological determination, followed quickly. Council policies soon became council theologies. By then the fate of the Franciscans was sealed.[38]

VII. JOHN EBERLIN OF GÜNZBURG: REFORM AND REACTION

INTRODUCTION

The most vigorous proponent of the Lutheran cause to emerge from the South German Franciscan Province was John Eberlin of Günzberg. Eberlin was not one of the young clerics who joined Luther's entourage. Although his birth date cannot be established with certainty, Eberlin was at least in his fifties and perhaps in his sixties when he left his position as *lector* in the friary in Ulm in 1521.[1] In the next four years, Eberlin released a torrent of pamphlets attacking his former order. He expounded his new-found creed eagerly but much of his energy was reserved for denunciations of the order to which he had formerly sworn obedience.

Eberlin's career until 1521 did not enjoy the spotlight of prominence which illuminated it thereafter. Only the scantiest biographical outline is available. He studied at various times at the Universities of Ingolstadt, Basel, and Freiburg in Breisgau. In 1519, he was forced to abandon his position as friary preacher in Tübingen. Eberlin's own account of his dismissal, written after he had left the order, claimed that the Tübingen doctors of theology moved to dismiss him because they were jealous of the popular following drawn to his preaching.[2]

No sooner had Eberlin been transferred to the position of *lector* in Ulm, than he became embroiled in an even more serious controversy. Because of his open advocacy of the Lutheran cause, his fellow friars forced him to leave. Again, in his post-Reformation writings, Eberlin pictured this dismissal as a monkish plot contravening popular sentiment. Specifically, he claimed that the City Council attempted without success to intervene on his behalf.[3] None of the genial spirit of Pellican was in Eberlin's breast after his departure from Ulm. Far from searching for any compromise between the friary and Lutheran teaching, Eberlin immediately launched his harsh attacks on the order. Within six months of his June, 1521, departure from the order, the *Fünfzehn Bundsgenossen* were published in Basel castigating the mendicant traditions.[4]

Eberlin traveled extensively through South Germany as he preached and wrote in support of the Lutheran cause. He studied with Luther at Wittenberg in 1522. Married in 1524, he was appointed pastor and superintendent by Count George II of Wertheim am Main who had declared for the evangelical cause. After the death of Count George in 1530, Eberlin was removed by a pro-Catholic regime. In the three remaining years of his life, he never found a satisfactory position. He ended his career "poor, neglected, disillusioned, embittered, irascible and crippled with gout. . . ."[5]

EBERLIN'S CONVERSION

Because of the paucity of information one can only speculate about Eberlin's intellectual orientation before 1521. The Freiburg of his university days knew firsthand of the peasants' revolt in the countryside. Some of the reforms he advocated in the *Fünfzehn Bundsgenossen* were later demanded by Schwabian peasants in the twelve articles published in Memmingen in 1524.[6]

Humanist influences were also prominent in his university days, especially at Basel. In 1526 Eberlin began the translation of Tacitus's *Germania* in order to enlighten his fellow countrymen regarding their origins.[7] This effort notwithstanding, Eberlin cannot be counted with Murner as one who sought to synthesize mendicant theology with a broad range of humanist learning. His critique of mendicant sermons in the *Fünfzehn Bundsgenossen* included a direct attack on the introduction of mathematical or grammatical illusions into preaching.[8] Eberlin called for a simple, direct, Biblical

---

[38] Alfred Schultze noted that with the coming of the Reformation, city councils first began to intervene in affairs of doctrine. See Schultze, *op. cit.*, pp. 26–29.

[1] Susan Groag Bell, "Johan Eberlin von Günzburg's *Wolfaria*: The First Protestant Utopia," *Church History* **36** (1967): pp. 122, 123.

[2] John Eberlin of Günzburg, "Syben frum aber trostloss pfaffen klagen ire not, einer dem anderen und ist niemant der sye tröste, Gott erbarme sich jre" (1522), *Sämtliche Schriften*, edited by Ludwig Enders, in: Flugschriften aus der Reformationszeit **15**, 2 (Halle, 1900): pp. 70, 71; hereafter cited as "Syben."

Among the doctors Eberlin listed as opponents was the famous Jacob Lemp. See Heinrich Hermelink, *Die Theologische Fakultät in Tübingen vor der Reformation* (Tübingen, 1906), pp. 83, 84.

[3] John Eberlin of Günzburg, "Die ander getrew vermanung Johannis Eberlin vonn Güntzberg, an der Rath der lobichen stadt Ulm. . ." (1523), *Sämtliche Schriften*, edited by Ludwig Enders, in: Flugschriften aus der Reformationszeit **18**, 3 (Halle, 1902): pp. 2, 3, 39, 40; hereafter cited as "Ulm."

[4] Eberlin's fifteen proposals were published with separate title pages for each, e.g., "Der erst bundtsgnoss" etc. See his *Sämtliche Schriften*, edited by Ludwig Enders, in: Flugschriften aus der Reformationszeit **11**, 1 (Halle, 1896): pp. 1–205; hereafter cited as "Bundtsgnoss."

[5] Bell, *op. cit.*, pp. 123, 124. Cf. Riggenbach, *Eberlin*, pp. 246–284.

[6] Bell, *op. cit.*, p. 131.

[7] *Ibid.*, p. 125.

[8] "Bundtsgnoss," pp. 56, 57.

sermon. On this point, Eberlin, the reformer, agreed with Schatzgeyer, the counter-reformer. Meanwhile, Murner and Pellican shared a receptivity for humanist learning although they came to opposite conclusions regarding Reformation theology.

Eberlin's own descriptions of his acceptance of Lutheranism are more tendentious than they are insightful. During his stay in Ulm, exposure to Luther's writings revolutionized his life and thought.[9] In his longest discussion of his change of mind written from Wittenberg in 1523, Eberlin was concerned to defend his own credibility. He conceded to his former audience in Tübingen that he had defended the "old" theology and mendicant rules with great vigor. He made a point of boasting about the following he had gathered in Tübingen.

By 1523, his problem was to preserve his credibility while declaring openly that his previous sermons had been in error. He argued that he had been trapped in a system of friary rules and sanctions which had blinded his eyes to the truth of the gospel. Now having seen the light, he wrote to warn others not to become subject to the wiles of Franciscan preachers.[10]

Unlike Pellican, Eberlin made no claim that his adoption of Reformation thought had its roots in his own thinking before he began to read Luther. His apologia painted a picture of sharp contrast. He was freed from the darkness of blind subjection as a friar to the light of the gospel. Ever eager to represent himself as the popular preacher who won the confidence of the multitudes, he sought to make a virtue out of the radicality of his change of heart.

THE FÜNFZEHN BUNDSGENOSSEN

Eberlin began his new career as a Protestant preacher and pamphleteer with the publication of the *Fünfzehn Bundsgenossen*. Although he devoted two chapters to general social and political reform, to the structuring of a *Wohlfaria*, one cannot conclude that he had become a political scientist instead of a theologian. Eberlin still conceived of society primarily in religious terms even if many of his motifs were negative. Above all else, he was concerned with the place of the priesthood and religious mores in society. He was determined to purge society of the religious pattern which had gripped it and to which he had been subject. Indeed, Eberlin displayed a compulsive animus about his own career, constantly returning to bitter criticism of the mendicant orders.

His call for reform was addressed to the emperor. He urged the emperor to alter the coterie of clerics from whom he received advice, suggesting that he replace the pernicious friars in his court with the likes of Erasmus, Luther, and Carlstadt as confessors.

Further, he played on the German animosity toward Italy and the pervasive feeling that German money was uselessly drained off to the papal court. He called for the presentation of evengelical truths in German so that the German layman could see through the fabrications which had been woven by the papal and mendicant cabal. Echoes of the *Reformatio Sigismundi* and of the writings of Marsilius of Padua are discernible in his proposals.[11]

Eberlin dramatized the financial impact of the mendicant orders on Germany by citing specific figures. The Observant Franciscans in Germany alone enjoyed an income of two hundred thousand gulden annually, he charged, while all the mendicant orders together accounted for an annual income of one million gulden. The papacy, he claimed, drained three hundred thousand gulden out of Germany each year.[12]

The mendicant orders, in sum, were viewed by Eberlin as a part of the papal plot to keep Germany in subjection and continue to bleed it financially. Therefore, he sought as a first priority that German princes free the country from this enslavement. He urged the emperor to turn the tables on Italy by marching into Rome and overseeing the reform of the papal curia.[13]

Eberlin's political and social utopia was only hastily outlined. Agricultural work was to be the basis of the economy and society. Classes that had previously stood above the peasants were now to join them in their work. Salaried public officials were to be elected. Social services such as a welfare system and public education were to occupy the special attention of these officials. The social services, available to all, were to be supported by all members of society.[14]

Eberlin's ideal state concerned itself with private as well as public morality. The social regulation of marriage was of special interest to Eberlin since he had experienced so keenly the conflicts of first being denied marriage and then proceeding to marry in the face of widespread disapproval. Hence, he emphasized that once young people had reached the majority, there should be no restrictions against their freedom to enter into marriage. The maintenance of chastity was to be totally voluntary.[15]

Eberlin was not as rigorous in his demands as the popular friar preachers of the fifteenth century had been. John of Capistrano had demanded that chessboards and cards be burned. Eberlin forbade such diversions to the young but permitted them for the old so long as they did not lead to excessive gambling. Likewise, regular public dances were to be organized.[16] Even the tone of Eberlin's attitude toward the Jewish

---

[9] Riggenbach, *Eberlin*, p. 15.
[10] John Eberlin of Günzburg, "Wider die falschscheynende gaystlichen under dem Christlichen haussen, genant Barfüsser oder Franciscaner orden. . ." (1523), edited by Ludwig Enders, *op. cit.* **18**, 3: pp. 68, 69. *Cf.* "Syben," pp. 70, 71.
[11] "Bundtsgnoss," pp. 80–88. *Cf.* Hans H. Ahrens, *Die religiösen, nationalen und sozialen Gedanken Johann Eberlin von Günzburgs* (Hamburg, 1939), pp. 42, 43.
[12] "Bundtsgnoss," p. 7.
[13] *Ibid.*, p. 13.
[14] *Ibid.*, pp. 122–131.
[15] *Ibid.*, p. 113.
[16] *Ibid.*, p. 124.

minority was considerably milder than that of the friar preachers. Even though they were not to be given citizenship rights, they were to be treated in a friendly manner.[17]

If Eberlin's political utopia was only vaguely sketched out, his ecclesiastical utopia was spelled out in considerable detail. The priest was to assume a less aloof role in society. Priests were to adopt lay clothing. They were to be free to marry like lay people. Further, they should be allowed to lay aside and resume their priestly office as they themselves chose. They were to be subject to the secular legal process as were all other citizens. Handcrafts and honest labor were not to be considered below their dignity.[18] In sum, the priesthood was to be much more open to lay society and more intermingled with it than it had been previously. Most importantly, religious orders were to be reformed or perhaps even abolished. Nunneries, he complained, served no useful role in society. He advised parents that it was better for their daughters to marry into lower social classes than to take vows. Even the proper religious training of young women was neglected in many nunneries, he complained.[19]

Eberlin's bitterness against the religious orders knew no bounds. He warned society that it should not rest with the idle confidence that the prayers and presence of the regular clergy within society guaranteed divine favor upon the entire community. To the contrary, Eberlin saw the religious houses so entwined in evil that instead of bringing divine favor to the community they induced divine wrath in the form of hail and storm and pestilence.[20]

The catalog of evil perpetrated by the mendicants was endless. Mendicant preachers were pests in Eberlin's view because they competed with and chased away the good preachers in the Church.[21] He accused the mendicants of having reduced the sacramental system to a money raising scheme. The mendicants' burial rites and anniversary masses were swindles, he charged, playing on the desire of relatives to further the spiritual state of their deceased relatives. He alleged that in some cases friaries did not faithfully observe the elaborate calendar of anniversary masses to which they were committed.[22]

Eberlin totally rejected the notion that the Observant reform had solved the problems present in the Franciscan order. The rule of St. Francis was in the beginning not divinely inspired and further had not been followed by later generations within the order. He viewed the reform movements as one failure after another. Each depended on its respective papal bull rather than returning to the original spirit of St. Francis who, for example, engaged willingly in hand labor.[23] In Eberlin's judgment the reforming efforts of the past century had completely missed the mark.

After ranting endlessly against religious orders, Eberlin prescribed the following changes. First, the present inhabitants of religious houses were to be given complete freedom to abandon their vows and special clothing and to reenter the lay world. There, they were to be treated with full respect, not as turncoats or failures. They were to be free to marry and their marriages were to be held in respect by all.

As to the future of the institutions themselves, religious houses were to be closed or to carry on a most attenuated existence. The mendicant houses, he said, should be closed down as public nuisances. Other houses might continue to exist provided they served some useful role in society such as providing education or lodging and care for the poor and aged. The inhabitants of religious houses were not to wear special clothing or to claim any more elevated spiritual role. They should be free to seek secular employment if they wished. All of the special exemptions and privileges, secular as well as ecclesiastical, were to be stripped from the houses. If any house was in need of reform, none of the old temporizing would do. Secular authorities should move in, close the house down and sequester its property. In fact, Eberlin urged public officials to oversee religious houses to make sure that they did not fall back into their old, evil ways. Stripped of their power, wealth, and special prerogatives, religious houses were either to disappear or to play a far different and far less important role within society.[24]

This reform, indeed revolution, within the Church was to be spearheaded by the simple layman. Eberlin accused the clerics and theologians of leading the Church into error. Now it was the responsibility of the simple layman to read the gospels and St. Paul in order to restore the Church to the truth in which it had lived during its first millennium. Only the most recent centuries had witnessed the Church's fall into error. Now the simple layman, not the clergy or hierarchy or religious orders, had the capacity to restore the Church to its pristine state.[25]

Eberlin's first venture into popular pamphleteering was an intensely personal, agonizing argument in support of the decision he had made. His laying aside of the Franciscan habit was not merely a religious decision. The thrust of his argument was to emphasize the political and social involvement of the religious houses. Just as Eberlin could begin an evangelical life only by leaving the friary so also a new and better society could be created only if the power of these houses was broken.

His arguments spoke quite directly to members of city councils, perturbed and uncertain regarding the religious policy they should pursue. First, his argument that reform of society began with reform of the

---

[17] *Ibid.*, pp. 130, 131.
[18] *Ibid.*, pp. 110, 111.
[19] *Ibid.*, pp. 25–28.
[20] *Ibid.*, p. 104.
[21] *Ibid.*, pp. 48, 49.
[22] *Ibid.*, pp. 68–75.

[23] *Ibid.*, pp. 96–99.
[24] *Ibid.*, pp. 112, 113, 134–141. *Cf.* Bell, *op. cit.*, p. 126.
[25] *Ibid.*, pp. 164–169.

Church gave them ample justification for their intervention in ecclesiastical affairs. Eberlin's proposals of 1521 were a surprisingly accurate reflection of policies that were pursued in city after city. The clergy and religious houses were stripped of their special prerogatives and public officials took responsibility for the overseeing of religious affairs. Eberlin understood quite correctly that the upheaval which was the Reformation involved a revising of political and social structures as well as ecclesiastical affairs.

CONTINUING REFORM

The Eberlin who published the *Fünfzehn Bundsgenossen* seemed ready to support major revolution within Germany. However, as the course of events became more radical, Eberlin quickly turned more conservative. Influenced strongly by his study in Wittenberg in 1522, Eberlin soon became a firm opponent of the Radical Reformation as well as the peasants' revolt. As was true of so many of his colleagues, Eberlin found himself attempting to put out the fire rather than fan it.

Still, his writings after 1521 had not lost all of their revolutionary zeal. The friars continued to be his favorite whipping boys. In a 1523 advisory to the City Council of Ulm, Eberlin detailed his charges against the friar orders. The friars, he alleged, were not satisfied to quarrel only among themselves. They succeeded in projecting their own disputes into divisions within society as a whole. Hence, in Eberlin's view, the continued existence of the friaries would guarantee divisions within the body politic.[26]

Eberlin cited further examples of the gap between pretention and reality within the houses. He questioned the sincerity of the friars' motivation in celebrating anniversary masses. Eberlin contended that when houses lost the income from anniversary masses, they failed to continue the celebration faithfully. Money, not pastoral care, was their real motivation.[27] Likewise, he claimed that in spite of all the verbiage to the contrary, men and women in religious orders were attracted to each other in violation of their vows. Such couples should be encouraged to accept the divinely ordained responsibilities of marriage.[28]

Eberlin wrote feelingly of the crisis of vocation which he and many of his colleagues were experiencing. The yearning for marriage felt by the priest need not be frustrated, he argued. He called on Christian society to accept the priest and particularly his wife hospitably, not to disdain them as religious or social truants. Further, he described the priest's desire to bridge some of the distance which had been created between priests and common people. For instance, he saw no convincing reasons why priests should not participate with other men in laboring with their hands. The lessening of the distinction between the priesthood and lay people was not merely a sound requirement but something many priests even desired.[29]

Finally, Eberlin reasserted even more vigorously the theme of the layman's right to participate in theological discussion. Popes and councils, Eberlin said, were subject to judgment by the word of God. Since every Christian is free to read the Bible, all the faithful can make determinations regarding the decrees of popes and councils. Nor should simple laymen defer to the authority of councils or learned theologians. Eberlin totally refused the notion that the layman should suspend judgment until the council had spoken. The coming of faith to the layman did not wait for the convening of the council. The layman with the guidance of scripture was free to proceed to his own decisions. As to theological expertise, Eberlin declared that all true Christians were learned men in matters of faith. They need not be subjected to a theological elite.[30]

EBERLIN'S REACTION

The atmosphere of Wittenberg in 1522 calmed Eberlin's revolutionary tendencies. Wirting in that year, Eberlin used the prestigious images of Luther, Melanchthon, and Carlstadt to appeal for quiet. Warning against the misuse of Christian freedom, Eberlin informed his South German readers that Luther still lived in the friary and wore the habit. He carefully avoided eating meat on Friday and other fast days, Eberlin noted. The same caution was true of Luther's colleagues. Thus, Eberlin concluded that the Christian freedom of Wittenberg was not the freedom to seek provocation and disruption. Instead, the evangelical Christian should be concerned in love for the unity of his fellow believers.[31]

Likewise Eberlin softened his stand on the continued existence of religious houses. In 1523 he wrote against any indiscriminate mass exodus from religious houses. He impressed on his readers the seriousness of a decision either to enter or to leave a religious house and warned against impetuous changes. Further he conceded that Christian freedom did not forbid life in a religious order. However, he cautioned anyone contemplating the vow to examine very carefully the obligations which he would accept. The evangelical reform of religious houses, not their abolition, had now become the major motif of Eberlin's writings.[32] The animus of his earlier

---

[26] "Ulm," pp. 9, 10.
[27] *Ibid.*, p. 23.
[28] *Ibid.*, p. 33.

[29] "Syben," pp. 59–66. *Cf.* John Eberlin of Günzburg, "Ein freundlichs zuschreyben an alle stendt teutscher nation. . ." (1524), edited by Ludwig Enders, *op. cit.* **18**, 3: pp. 141–143.
[30] John Eberlin of Günzburg, "Ein büchlin dar in auff drey fragen geantwurt wirt" (1523), edited by Ludwig Enders, *op. cit.* **15**, 2: pp. 166–169, 181.
[31] John Eberlin of Günzburg, "Von misbrauch Christlicher freyheyt" (1522), edited by Ludwig Enders, *op. cit.* **15**, 2: pp. 44, 45. *Cf.* Eberlin's "Wie sich eyn diener Gotteswortts ynn all seynem thun halten soll" (1525), edited by Ludwig Enders, *op. cit.* **18**, 3: p. 211; hereafter cited as "Diener."
[32] John Eberlin of Günzburg, "Wider den unfürsichtigen unbeschanden aussganng viler der klosterleüt aus iren klöstern. . ." (1523), edited by Ludwig Enders, *op. cit.* **15**, 2: pp. 123–125, 133–136.

attacks against religious orders was replaced by a more cautious and considered judgment of religious houses.

Both the spread of the Radical Reformation and the threat of the peasants' war pressured Eberlin to assume an even more conservative stance. In late 1521 or early 1522, Eberlin had written a treatise espousing some of Carlstadt's opinions. Eberlin attacked the excessive dependence of the Church upon those physical symbols which had their proper place in the old covenant. Holy water and expensive altarware and even a physical understanding of the Eucharist were to be rejected in the age of the spirit.[33]

Eberlin's attraction to Carlstadt's ideas was temporary. During his stay in Wittenberg, he opted for Luther's direction rather than that of Carlstadt. He intended his attack on the misuse of Christian freedom as an attack against the burgeoning Radical Reformation.[34]

Eventually Eberlin faced the threat of the peasants' revolt near at hand. In 1524, in Erfurt, he began to preach against a radicalization of the Reformation which would lead to revolt in society.[35] Fearing a peasants' uprising, Eberlin totally disowned any alliance with their movement which may have been implied in the *Fünfzehn Bundsgenossen*. By 1526, Eberlin was advocating a conservative, class-structured view of society. He cautioned his readers against rebellion and uproar and informed them that it was their Christian duty to obey the classes set above them.[36]

In theology as well as social theory, Eberlin became more and more conservative. In an instruction to evangelical ministers written in 1524, Christian freedom was defined in most conservative terms. Evangelical Christians were urged to tolerate and accept everything which did not interfere with faith in Christ. The minimum, not the maximum of revolution, was called for. Within three short years Eberlin had concluded that the radicals were worse enemies than the Catholics. He remarked that he would rather preach in a city full of papists than a city full of uproarious radicals.[37] He feared more the new threat of uproar than he did the old threat of that power which had dismissed him from Ulm.

Eberlin had moved quickly from creating utopias to putting down revolts. As was true of his evangelical colleagues, Eberlin found it much harder to create the new order than it had been to escape from the oppressive power of the old. He was more concerned with the uncontrolled forces released by the Reformation than he was by the oppressive power of the old order.

Facing the threat of a peasants' rebellion, Eberlin no longer proposed secular utopias. To the contrary, he warned his readers that their Christian duty was to seek a spiritual utopia outside of this world. This world is a prison, he said, ruled by tyrants who serve at the pleasure of God. The evangelical message is not one of overthrow but rather one of patience in this world and expectation of a perfect order hereafter. Hence, it is the responsibility of evangelical Christians to obey their rulers, imperfect as they may be.[38] Eberlin had come very nearly full circle. His late writings lack only the admonition that the patient Christian army in this world, expecting a new order hereafter, should be led by an elite of devout men pledged to patience in this world, namely followers of the rule of St. Francis.

VIII. THE BEGINNINGS OF THE COUNTER REFORMATION

THE TRAGIC END OF MURNER'S CAREER

As a man with ample appetite for literary battle, Murner seemed ideally suited to engage in the bitter polemics stirred up by the Reformation. However, far from prospering in this period of conflict, Murner's career came to a tragic end. His harsh tactics earned so much enmity that he was banned from city after city. In the last years before his death in 1535, Murner lived in isolation in his place of birth, Oberrehnheim. Cut off from the cultural activity of the more prosperous cities, Murner had been driven out of any major role in the Reformation controversy.

After his initial attempts to remonstrate with Luther had been rebuffed, Murner resorted to hostile criticism of the Reformers. Instead of analyzing Luther's theology, Murner pointed to the social and institutional consequences of the spread of the Reformation. Repeatedly, he insisted that the peasants' revolt was the result of the new doctrines.[1] The Reformers, he insisted, had no basis in *"Recht"* for their assertions and actions. For example, their attempt to establish a scriptural authority was unsatisfactory because, in Murner's view, Scripture could never be self-explanatory. Interpretive responsibility was required and hence a hierarchical system was necessary. If the Reformers were to point to the council, then Murner countered

---

[33] John Eberlin of Günzburg, "Wider die schender der Creaturen gottes..." (1525), edited by Ludwig Enders, *op. cit.* 15, 2: pp. 1–19. Cf. Riggenbach, *Eberlin*, pp. 82–97.

[34] Riggenbach, *Eberlin*, pp. 109, 110.

[35] *Ibid.*, pp. 210–245, especially pp. 231–233.

[36] John Eberlin of Günzburg, "Ein getrewe warnung an die Christen in der Burgawischen marck..." (1526), edited by Ludwig Enders, *op. cit.* 18, 3: pp. 255–287; hereafter cited as "Warnung." Cf. Kyle C. Sessions, "Christian Humanism and Freedom of a Christian: Johann Eberlin von Günzburg to the Peasants," in: *The Social History of the Reformation*, edited by Lawrence P. Buck and Jonathan W. Zophy (Columbus, 1972), pp. 137–155. Sessions is quite correct in emphasizing the conservative tone of this document. However, his failure to analyze earlier writings by Eberlin deprives the reader of the awareness that this caution was the final stage of a volatile career.

[37] "Diener," pp. 211, 212.

[38] "Warnung," pp. 261, 262, 276–280.

[1] Thomas Murner, "Hie würt angezeigt das unchristlich frevel, ungelört und unrechtlich ussriessen und fürnemen einer loblichen herrschafft von Bern ein disputation zu halten..." (1528), edited by Wolfgang Pfeiffer-Belli in *Thomas Murner in Schweizer Glaubenskampf*, in: Corpus Catholicorum 22 (Münster/W., 1939): pp. 49, 53; hereafter cited as "Bern." Cf. Murner's "Von dem grossen Lutherischen Narren," edited by Paul Merker in *Thomas Murners Deutsche Schriften* (Strassburg, 1931) 9: pp. 214–221; hereafter cited as "Narren."

that from the very beginning of the Church, the pope had held supremacy over the council.[2] In sum, Murner painted the Reformers as irresponsible radicals who had torn away completely from any moorings of institutional responsibility. Disastrous turmoil and anarchy would accrue to Christian society if the Reformers' lead were followed.

Murner's indictment of the Reformers was expressed most sharply in his poetry. His development of the literary theme of the fool which he had adopted from Sebastian Brant found its final development in his attack on the Reformers in his poem of 1522, "Von dem grossen Lutherischen Narren." Before the Reformation, Murner used the image of the fool to describe man as not merely blind but sinful and demonic. Now in the Reformers, Murner saw the most serious embodiment of this motif. He pictured the Reformers as sinfully rebellious individualists rejecting the divinely established and time-proven institutions of the Church. Their discussion of the gospel he saw as an attempt to assert their demonic control over the divine word.

John Eberlin's Utopia was Thomas Murner's hell. Precisely those institutions and regulations which kept down the demonic individualism of men were thrown overboard by Eberlin. Charging them with attempting to establish themselves as autonomous men, Murner saw the Reformers as the most dangerous kinds of fools. In his work they took on a titanic character as they threatened to destroy the divinely ordained system.[3]

Murner closed his "Lutherischen Narren" on a bitter personal note. Luther was represented as offering his daughter's hand in marriage to Murner provided that the prospective groom become a Lutheran. Having accepted the terms, Murner was portrayed as reciting the creed which he now embraced. Pope and emperor, Church and sacraments, priests and friars all fell by the wayside. The creed was wholly negative. The Christian freedom of Luther meant that all of this was sworn off.

Having made the bargain, Murner proceeded lustfully to claim his prize. The bridal dinner and dance were portrayed as bereft of grace and style. No ecclesiastical blessing was invoked. Luther's freedom, as portrayed by the poem, unleashed the basest qualities in man. Once the crude preliminaries were completed, Murner led his bride to bed. There to his horror, he discovered that she was diseased. He promptly renounced the marriage noting that no sacrament was involved anyway. Luther was portrayed as so shocked by the discovery that he was driven to his death bed where life ended without the comfort of the sacrament. Thus did Luther's rebellion come to a fitting end.[4]

Murner's tragic pilgrimage began with his departure from Strassburg in 1524. He left for Oberrehnheim and was forbidden by the city of Strassburg to return lest he disturb the peace there.[5] The next year the peasants' revolt engulfed Oberrehnheim and Murner fled to Lucerne, a Catholic stronghold in Switzerland. Immediately, Murner established himself as a protagonist for the Catholic side. Within the next two years, he participated in the great Swiss disputations at Baden and Bern. Again in 1529, fearing that his life was threatened by the religious war in Switzerland, Murner fled to Oberrehnheim. There he lived until his death in 1537 as an exile, hostage to the divisiveness of the period. Banned from Strassburg and fearful for his safety in the Swiss cities, Murner was no longer an influential writer. Even at the great Diet of Augsburg in 1530, his services were not called for because he was too controversial a figure to be useful at a moment when compromise was being sought.[6]

In his youth, Murner had traversed Latin Christendom freely studying theology and humanistic topics. By the end of his life, the fracturing effects of the Reformation had left its impact not only on the political geography of Europe but also on the patterns of theological and intellectual intercourse. So controversial a writer as Murner found himself exiled from the great urban cultural centers of Germany. Murner's last years of isolation in Oberrehnheim symbolized the destruction of the theological and intellectual universalism of European society.[7]

THE SPOKESMAN FOR THE COUNTER REFORMATION IN BAVARIA: FROM MEDIATION TO COUNTER REFORMATION

The Counter Reformation as a self-conscious movement began only after the depth of the impact of the Reformation was clear. At first the Reformers were misjudged by the established Church because they were viewed either as too benign or too evil. Schatzgeyer, for example, had at first considered some compromise a realistic possibility. John Eck, on the other hand, sought simply to dismiss the Reformers as heretics who deserved their fate. But the problem posed by the Reformation was not to be solved by either of these approaches.

In addition to Murner, whose tactics had made him so unwanted, the leading spokesman for the Catholic cause in the South German Province became Caspar Schatzgeyer. After finishing his second term as pro-

---

[2] Thomas Murner, "Ein brieff der strengen eren not festen Fursuhtigen Ersamen wysen der XII örter einer löbischen eydtgnoschafft" (1526), edited by Pfeiffer-Belli, in: Corpus Catholicorcum 22: pp. 3, 4; hereafter cited as "Brieff." See also his "Ein worhaftigs verantwurten der hochgelorten doctores und herren" (1526) edited by Pfeiffer-Belli, *Idem.*, pp. 25, 26; hereafter cited as "Verantwurten." *Cf.* Murner's "An der Grossmechtigsten und Durchlüchtigsten adel tütscher nation. . ." (1520), edited by Pfeiffer-Belli in *Thomas Murners Deutsche Schriften* (Berlin and Leipzig, 1928) 6: p. 88.

[3] Könneker, *op. cit.*, pp. 185–203. For Murner's critique of Eberlin's Fünfzehn Budtsgnossen see his "Narren," pp. 122–165.

[4] "Narren," pp. 239–266. For the editor's comments on the bitter tone of this section see Merker's introduction, pp. 56, 57.

[5] Liebenau, *op. cit.*, p. 210.

[6] *Ibid.*, pp. 248–253.

[7] A thorough discussion of this point can be found in Friedrich Heer, *Die Dritte Kraft: Der europaische Humanismus zwischen den Fronten des Konfessionellen Zeitalters* (Frankfurt/M., 1960).

vincial (1520–1523) Schatzgeyer returned to Munich where he devoted the last four years of his life to defense of traditional Catholicism and more exactly, traditional religious orders.

Schatzgeyer had none of the explosive personal qualities of an Eck or a Murner. In fact his contemporaries commented that he was a gentle and compassionate man.[8] Hence, his work was characterized by neither scorn nor venom. In his *Scrutinium* he had attempted to mediate between the Reformers and their opponents. Even after he realized that mediation was impossible, his writings continued to analyze carefully the conflicts between the Reformation and traditional teachings. Although he came to reject the Reformers' positions, he paid them the compliment of taking them seriously.

Many factors entered into Schatzgeyer's conversion to a Counter Reformation point of view. The confrontation in Basel was not the only rebuff which Schatzgeyer faced when he attempted to mediate the dispute. Luther totally rejected Schatzgeyer's moderate tone in the *Scrutinium*. Schatzgeyer had entitled each section of that work a *conatus,* that is, an attempt to find a *via media* for each issue in conflict. Luther threw this language back in Schatzgeyer's face by replying that it was to be sure an "attempt," an attempt to reconcile Christ and Belial, Holy Scripture and the sacrilege of scholastic theology.[9]

Further, Luther's publication of *De votis monasticis* hardened Schatzgeyer's attitude. The *Scrutinium* was published in March, 1522. Shortly thereafter, Schatzgeyer read Luther's attack on religious orders and by the summer of the same year was writing his *Replica,* a defense of religious orders. Whereas Schatzgeyer's own "Lutheran" friend, Pellican, was eager to keep his place within the order, Luther was providing a public rationale for departure from religious orders and the closing of their houses. Between the *Scrutinium* and the *Replica* there was a marked change of tone. Within the corpus of Schatzgeyer's writings this was the time when he clearly joined the Counter Reformation.[10]

Finally, Schatzgeyer's last years were spent in a political environment which suppressed Lutheranism with increasing vigor. The dukes of Bavaria, Wilhelm and Ludwig, temporized when Lutheran influences first appeared in Bavaria. But just as Schatzgeyer completed his second tour of duty as provincial (1523) and returned to Munich, the dukes became determined to uproot Lutheranism. Indeed, from the very beginning the dukes' chancellor, Leonhard von Eck, had urged a hard line against the followers of Luther.[11]

In 1523 the dukes had very carefully supervised the action taken against Arsacius Seehofer, a professor at the University of Ingolstadt, who had studied in Wittenberg with Melancthon and was now accused of Lutheran teachings. Schatzgeyer participated in the attack against Seehofer by authorizing the publication of a denounciation of his teachings.[12]

The posthumous publication of Schatzgeyer's *Opera Omnia* in Ingolstadt in 1543 was set in this political context of the Counter Reformation. Two introductory letters were provided. One was written by John Eck and the other by John Bachman, the preacher at the Ingolstadt friary. Both letters hailed Schatzgeyer as an exponent of the true faith. John Eck noted that Schatzgeyer was a quiet and peaceable man but Eck left no hint that his teachings had ever been less than orthodox. In fact he pictured Schatzgeyer as a contemporary St. Augustine fending off the heretics with the sharpness of his pen. Bachman wrote his letter as a commendation of Schatzgeyer's works to the chancellor, Leonhard von Eck, and to Duke Wilhelm of Bavaria.

The dukes of Bavaria placed a letter of commendation at the end of Schatzgeyer's opus. They instructed the clergy throughout their lands to purchase copies of this work and to utilize it as a statement of true Christian doctrine. Thus Schatzgeyer's writings were held up by the dukes as a definitive formulation of Catholic doctrine for the Counter Reformation in Bavaria.[13]

Finally, Schatzgeyer's writings did nothing to ease the minds of the Bavarian politicians regarding the tie between Lutherans and Anabaptists. The dukes' chancellor had insisted that the peasants' revolt was a natural consequence of Lutheran teachings. The appearance of Anabaptists within Bavaria frightened the dukes into their most severe actions against dissident teachings.[14] Schatzgeyer only helped to blur the distinctions between Lutherans and Anabaptists by his writings. In his last defense of the sacraments he listed certain teachings characteristic of the Anabaptists with certain "Lutheran" propositions, all of which he rejected.[15] This identification could only serve to con-

---

[8] John Eck's description of Schatzgeyer as calm and gentle is found in his letter of commendation placed at the beginning of Schatzgeyer's *Opera Omnia* (Ingolstadt, 1543). For Pellican's view of Schatzgeyer's personality see the author's "Caspar Schatzgeyer and Conrad Pellican. . .," pp. 187–190.

[9] See Luther's preface to John Brismann, *Ad Gasparis Schatzgeyri minoritae plicas responsio per Iohannem Brismann pro Lutherano libello de missis et votis monasticis* (Wittenberg, 1523). Other Reformers were equally harsh in their rejection of Schatzgeyer's attempts to mediate. See Paulus, *op. cit.,* pp. 49, 52, 80–82.

[10] Caspar Schatzgeyer, "Replica contra periculosa scripta post Scrutinium divine scripture iam pridem emissum emanata" (1522), cited from the *Opera Omnia* (Ingolstadt, 1543), hereafter cited as "Replica."

[11] Strauss, "The Religious Policies. . ." pp. 353, 358–362.

[12] *Ibid.,* p. 359. *Cf.* Karl Schottenloher, *Der Münchner Buchdrucker Hans Schobser, 1500–1530* (Munich, 1925), pp. 8, 9.

[13] The letters are found in the *Opera Omnia,* the first two after the table of contents and the dukes' letter just before the subject index.

[14] Strauss, "The religious Policies. . .," pp. 364–367.

[15] Caspar Schatzgeyer, "Ecclesiasticorum Sacramentorum assertio" (1530), cited from the *Opera Omnia,* 292k; hereafter cited as "Assertio."

firm the view of the dukes and their chancellor that all of the dissent moving through Bavaria sprang from one heretical root.

By the end of his career Schatzgeyer did not hesitate to label Lutheran teachings heretical. In his *Traductio Sathane* written in 1525, he declared that he would expose the diabolical deceit of the Lutherans. This heresy, like others before it, was necessary as a test of the truth of Catholic doctrine. Just as Satan transforms himself into an angel of light so that he might deceive, satanic doctrine presents itself as scriptural, and false apostles call themselves apostles of Christ. With this condemnation Schatzgeyer completely closed the door on any possibility of reconciliation.[16]

THE EUCHARISTIC DEBATE

As it became clear to Schatzgeyer that mediation was not possible, he moved away from a discussion of the Reformers' favorite locus—justification—to a defense of the Eucharist and religious orders as he had come to understand them. His defense of the Eucharist began in earnest in 1525 when he exchanged bitter pamphlets with Andreas Osiander.[17]

Osiander, following Luther's lead, focused the discussion on the concepts of sacrifice and testament. He contended that the concept of sacrifice implied that man offered something to God while the testament involved God's giving to man. Rejecting the notion of sacrifice, Osiander held that the Eucharist was best described as a testament in which God bestowed on man the forgiveness of sins.[18]

Schatzgeyer responded by seeking to clarify what he considered terminological confusion created by the Reformers. He said the testament, the totality of benefits left to the believers by Christ, embraced much more than the Eucharist alone. In his view, the testament included all of the benefits Christ declared while on the cross. Thus the concept of testament embraced the forgiveness of sins and the promise of paradise as well as the adoption as children of God and the promise of Christ's final victory.[19]

Distinct from the proclamation of the testament from the cross was Christ's sacrifice which established the Eucharist. By offering himself, Christ sealed and confirmed the work of his testament.[20] Although the testament and Eucharist are distinct concepts, they are nevertheless related. While the faithful celebrate the Eucharist, they are to recall the words of the testament.[21]

In like manner, Schatzgeyer took exception to the Reformers' insistence that forgiveness of sins was conferred with the Eucharist. He insisted that the Eucharist was instituted during the Last Supper before the shedding of blood on the cross had made available the forgiveness of sins.[22] This sharp distinction between the last meal and Christ's suffering on the cross which was introduced for polemical purposes, contained within it the potential for great difficulties. The Eucharistic sacrifice would simply be emptied of its content were it to refer only to the last meal. Although Schatzgeyer attempted to resolve this problem elsewhere,[23] his eagerness to refute the Reformers contributed to the imbalance of his own position.

Schatzgeyer sought to reaffirm in clear language still another point—the relation of the sacrifice on the altar to that which took place on Calvary. While denying that the Eucharist repeated the sacrifice on the cross, Schatzgeyer chose to speak of a "representation" or "renewal" of this sacrifice.[24]

Schatzgeyer was careful to emphasize that this terminology was not intended to spiritualize the real sacrifice of the mass. Quite specifically, he contrasted the spiritual offering of Christ in the devout meditation of the faithful with the solemn representation of Christ's sacrifice which takes place in the Eucharist. The spiritual remembrance is the task of the universal priesthood of believers while the ordained priesthood alone conducts the representation of Christ's sacrifice.[25] The Eucharist is a real offering, not mere remembrance. The significance of Christ's suffering becomes more forcefully and clearly present in this sacrament than it does in the spiritual devotion of all believers.[26]

The close bond between the sacrifice on the altar and the events on Calvary was adduced by Schatzgeyer to

---

[16] Caspar Schatzgeyer, "Traductio Sathanae" (written in 1525 but first published in 1530), *Opera Omnia*, pp. 247ff.

[17] Andreas Osiander, *Wider Caspar Schatzgeyer, Barfuser Münchs, unchristlichs schreyben, damit er dass die Messs eyn opffer sey, zu beweysen vermaint* (Nuremberg, 1525); hereafter cited as *Wider*. Schatzgeyer answered with his *Abwaschung des unflats so Andreas Osiander dem Gaspar Schatzger in sein antlitz gespiehen hat* (Landshut, 1525); hereafter cited as *Abwaschung*. Although Luther was not quoted directly the issues under debate were discussed by Luther in his "Ein Sermon von dem neuen Testament, das ist von der heiligen Messe" (1520), *WA* **6**: pp. 349–378 and "De captivitate Babylonica ecclesiae praeludium" (1520), *WA*, **6**: pp. 484–573.

[18] Osiander, *Wider*, B i, ii. For Luther's discussion of testament and sacrifice see his "Ein Sermon. . .," pp. 357–368. Cf. Kenneth Hagen, "From Testament to Covenant in the Early Sixteenth Century," *Sixteenth Century Journal* 3, 1 (1972): pp. 1–24.

[19] *Abwaschung*, A iv, A iv^v. Cf. Schatzgeyer's "Replica," 84 A - 85 F and his "Examen novarum doctrinarum" (1523), *Opera Omnia*, 188 E; hereafter cited as "Examen."

[20] "Replica," 85 G and "Examen" 128 Y.

[21] "Replica," 85 G.

[22] *Abwaschung*, B, C iv.

[23] "Assertio," 300 H.

[24] Caspar Schatzgeyer, "Tractatus de Missa'" (1525), *Opera Omnia*, 190 T - 192 H; hereafter cited as "Tractatus." For further discussion of this problem see Francis Clark, *Eucharistic Sacrifice and the Reformation* (London, 1960) and Erwin Iserloh, *Die Eucharistie in der Darstellung des Johannes Eck*, in: Reformationsgeschictliche Studien und Texte **73/74** (Münster/W., 1950).

[25] "Tractatus," 190-191 T; "Abwaschung," H iii - H iv. Cf. Erwin Iserloh's discussion of Schatzgeyer's writings in *Der Kampf um die messe in den ersten Jahren der Auseinandersetzung mit Luther*, in: Katholisches Leben und Kämpfen in Zeitalter der Glaubensspaltung **10** (Münster/W., 1952).

[26] "Assertio," 295 K, 299 B and "Ein gietliche und freuntliche anntwort" (1526), F ii: hereafter cited as "Anntwort."

refute the Reformers' charge that the interpretation of the Eucharist as sacrifice implied that the faithful were earning merit for themselves by offering up Christ. The meritorious fruits of the mass are not the result of man's work. They flow from Christ's sacrifice which is represented and renewed on the altar.[27]

Having thus defined the relation between the sacrament on the altar and the sacrifice on Calvary, Schatzgeyer drew his conclusions about the priesthood. Just as the sacrifice is not repeated on the altar, so the priests are not successors of Christ. Instead, the priests represent Christ when they offer the mass in his name.[28]

A striking contrast existed between Schatzgeyer's answer to the Reformers' discussion of the Eucharist as testament and his reaffirmation of the Eucharist as sacrifice. In the first instance he struggled, not wholly successfully, to provide a convincing refutation of the Reformers. His reaffirmation, on the other hand, represented a happy return to familiar ground. The argument is clear and coherent, not distorted by polemical emphases. His task was to take into account the Reformers' attacks but not be drawn onto their ground. Thus did he help formulate an emerging Counter Reformation theology.

THE DISTRIBUTION OF THE FRUITS OF THE MASS

No discussion of the Reformation controversy regarding the Eucharist would be complete without a comment on the practice of purchasing masses so that the fruits might be distributed to specified persons. The Reformers had chosen this practice as an object of criticism. Osiander, for instance, began his pamphlet against Schatzgeyer with the comment that the whole debate about the Eucharist in Nuremberg had been stirred up by the attack launched by the priors of St. Sebalt and St. Lorenz. These two leaders of the Nuremberg clergy had attacked the bazaarlike atmosphere surrounding the sale of Eucharistic celebrations.[29] Further, they pointed out that the practice of purchasing masses discriminated against the poor. They charged that the practice was carried on only for the income it generated.[30]

Luther attacked the traffic in masses on two counts. First he said such masses were based on the assumption that they were good works which earn a spiritual reward. In addition, this usage assumed that the spiritual fruit of the masses could be assigned to benefactors of religious houses as a repayment for their temporal gift.[31] Thus the sale of masses reinforced the notion that God required a certain quantity of merits and that these merits were transferable from one person to another. Luther insisted that the requirement of God—faith in his promises—could not be satisfied vicariously.[32]

Schatzgeyer, like Luther, did not approach this problem on the practical level. Rather, he discussed the theological presuppositions which underlay the practice of purchasing masses for specific persons. The ecclesiastical practice in this case had run ahead of the theological formulations. The practice of purchasing masses and assigning benefits to specific persons was based on the assumption that the fruits of the mass were finite and quantifiable. Because the benefits were finite the faithful requested a proliferation of masses. Still other problems were inherent in this view of the mass. For instance, it overemphasized the Church's role in the offering of Christ, neglecting the fact that Christ himself is the *"Principalis Offerens."* [33]

Schatzgeyer's emphasis on the unity between the sacrifice on Calvary and its repetition on the altar and his assertion that the priesthood serving at the altar represent Christ called into question the notion that a finite fruit resulted from the celebration of the mass. In addition Schatzgeyer asserted that what results from the mass is of no less effect than what was accomplished on the cross.[34]

This assertion alone does not cut away the foundations from the practice of the mass stipend and the request for special masses. In his discussion of the relation between the fruits of Christ's sufferings on the cross and the penitential practice of the Church, Schatzgeyer made clear that there was a distinction between the totality of the fruit resulting from Christ's death and the part of the fruit applied to each believer. The celebration of the mass does indeed provide satisfaction for sin but not total satisfaction. Christ, who by his suffering and death earned the satisfaction, distributes these merits to the faithful according to his good pleasure.[35]

Indeed Schatzgeyer defended masses for the dead on two counts. First, he said Christ can dispense the merits of his sufferings—how and where he will—to the living as well as to the dead.[36] Further, he pointed out that the unity of the body of Christ is not disrupted by death. It is only incidental to the unity of the Church and hence to the distribution of the fruits of the mass that some are living and some are departed.[37]

Hence Schatzgeyer should not be presented as having destroyed the rationale for the purchase of masses and the assignment of the fruits of masses to specific persons. Writing on a strictly theological level, he provided a justification for the continuing practice of

---

[27] "Replica," 80 Q - 81 R and "Anntwort," E iv.
[28] "Assertio," 300 G; "Replica," 82 V; "Tractatus," 191 T.
[29] Osiander, *Wider*, A iv.
[30] See above, ch. 6, fn 5.
[31] Martin Luther, "De votis monasticis Martini Lutheri iudicium" (1521), *WA* 8: p. 629.
[32] "De captivitate Babylonica," *WA* 6: p. 515.
[33] Erwin Iserloh, "Der Wert der Messe in der Diskussion der Theologen vom Mittelalter bis zum 16 Jahrhundert," *Zeitschrift für Katholische Theologie* 83 (1961): pp. 44, 67, 69.
[34] *Ibid.*, p. 77. *Cf.* "Tractatus," 192 C.
[35] "Tractatus," 201 Q.
[36] "Tractatus," 201 R.
[37] Schatzgeyer, *Vom fegfeur* (Munich, 1525), F, G iv.

specifying those persons who should benefit as a result of the celebration of the Eucharist.

RELIGIOUS ORDERS

Schatzgeyer's ultimate conflict with the Reformers concerned religious orders. Pellican, who sought to reconcile his Reformed theological outlook with continued allegiance to the Franciscan order, was the exception. Most of the other spokesmen for the Reformation leveled serious attacks against the religious orders. The debate continued after Schatzgeyer published his *Replica* in 1522. Although Luther contended that Schatzgeyer's effort had not refuted his arguments, he was pressed by friends to answer the Franciscan. Luther chose to commission a fellow theologian of Wittenberg, John Brismann, to carry out this task. Brismann was himself a former Franciscan who had earned his doctor of theology degree at Wittenberg in 1523.[38]. Answering Brismann, Schatzgeyer steadfastly defended religious vows.[39]

Of capital importance was the perspective from which Schatzgeyer discussed religious orders after the Reformers' attack. Just before the outbreak of the Reformation, Schatzgeyer had been a spokesman for a particular wing of the Franciscan order. He had bitter words for his foes, the Conventuals. Although he did not address himself to the question, his order had been caught up in the fierce Mariological controversy with the Dominicans.

In a dramatic shift of role, Schatzgeyer became a defender of religious orders in general. The foe was no longer a fellow member of his order with a different persuasion on internal questions. With the entire existence of his order and indeed all religious orders threatened, internal controversies were muted. The dispute no longer concerned comparative levels of strictness in observing one's vow. The question had become whether one should take a vow at all.

Schatzgeyer's role was symptomatic of the hardened defense lines which the Church drew up against the Reformation. The dissent and disputation within the medieval Church had been a part of its Catholicity, Even within the religious orders, very different views were in conflict with each other regarding the road by which one should seek to attain the perfect life and beatitude. Forced to the defensive by the onslaught of the Reformation, Schatzgeyer's writings came to defend a monolith of religious orders for which he proposed a common ideology.

Both Luther and his colleague, Brismann, attacked the religious elitism which was a presupposition of membership in religious orders. Luther objected to the suggestion that those subject to the vow were somehow more perfect Christians than the laity. This distinction was possible only when one measured perfection by ostentatious works.[40] Brismann pressed the point more explicitly. If life subject to the rule was the best way to beatitude, he asked, should not all Christians be advised to choose the path? Or is there indeed a distinction between those who seek perfection and those who strive for lesser goals?[41]

Schatzgeyer rejected the spiritual egalitarianism proposed by the Reformers. He divided the Christian community into three groups: the true (*verus*) Christians, the proven (*probatus*) Christians, and the perfect (*perfectus*) Christians. The minimum presupposition for the true Christian life is the mortification of the flesh and the destruction of the power of the old Adam in the spirit. The proven Christian has reformed his inner powers, his reason and desire. He presents to his fellows works of mercy and love. The perfect Christian, cleansed of all desire for lower objects, attains a state of perfect passivity and is ready for the influx of God into him.[42]

Schatzgeyer recognized the force of the Reformers' critique. He insisted that the quest for perfection was open to all Christians.[43] Still, the road to perfection is arduous and need not be required of all Christians.[44] Furthermore, the life of the laity is not, in practice, consistent with the attainment of perfection. Celibacy, Schatzgeyer insisted, was indispensable to the pursuit of the perfect life.[45] By living in a religious house one would find it easier to avoid the evils of the world and discover peace for contemplation.[46] Although the laity were not totally excluded from the contemplative life, they experienced a lesser form of its spiritual delight than did those who had devoted themselves totally to the quest for perfection under the guidance of a religious rule.[47]

In one of his last popular German writings published in 1527, Schatzgeyer dropped all hesitation to defend the superior spirituality of the regular orders. The life of perpetual chastity, he said, was to be considered better than the married state. Life in subjection to the vow offered a more certain path to the eternal reward than did the life of the layman. In sum, Schatzgeyer interpreted the gospels to declare that life under the vow was better and more blessed than the life of the laity.[48]

John Brismann, like John Eberlin, joined Luther in launching still another serious attack against the antisocial character of life in religious houses. They insisted that the penitential regime imposed on the orders

---

[38] See the editor's introduction to Luther's "De votis monasticis," *WA* **8**: p. 567.

[39] Schatzgeyer's continued defense of religious orders was contained in his "Examen" (1523) and his "De vita christiana et monastici instituti ad eam optima quadratura" (1524) cited from the *Opera Omnia;* hereafter referred to as "Vita."

[40] "De votis monasticis," *WA* **8**: p. 584.
[41] Brismann, *op. cit.*, 14ᵛ.
[42] "Replica," 51 I - 54 Y.
[43] "Examen," 111 C.
[44] "Replica," 56 L.
[45] *Ibid.*, 68 E.
[46] "Vita," 146 F.
[47] "Examen," 118 I, K.
[48] Schatzgeyer, *Wider Herr Hansen von Schwartzenbergs neulich aussgangen puechlin von der kirchendiener und gaystlichen personen* (Munich, 1527), K iii - K iv.

created a selfish spirituality. Luther charged that the penitential activity of the regular clergy accomplished nothing for the brother in need, and what is worse, it was offered as an excuse for neglecting those needs. Indeed in Luther's view, monastic obligations so debilitated the life of true Christian service that the two could not go together. He called on his reader to choose between the religious vow and the divine command to love one's neighbor.[49] Brismann added that love for one's neighbor should involve more than spiritual assistance. Even though the religious houses could claim that they contributed an overwhelming abundance of the spiritual wealth of the whole Church, that did not suffice. Physical works of love were also called for.[50]

Finally, John Eberlin attacked his former colleagues, the Observants, by insisting that they were incapable of performing acts of love for their neighbors. He pictured them as investing so much energy in celebration of their Observant ideals that they could accomplish little else.[51]

Schatzgeyer refused to tolerate any total abandonment of social responsibility. He pictured the penitential requirements imposed on man as including specific, external actions. But, he added, the interpersonal dimension should not be overemphasized. Man was created first of all for union with God and only secondarily for association with his fellows. Even if an individual were alone in the world he could alone march down the long road to the eternal reward.[52]

Schatzgeyer modified this radical individualism by reminding his reader that all Christians were members of the body of Christ. But as fellow members of the one body his emphasis was on the sharing of spiritual works and prayers rather than on physical works of love.[53] Schatzgeyer was less concerned about the society of pilgrims marching toward the heavenly city than he was about the progress the pilgrims made—individually or communally—toward the final goal. Concern for one's neighbor was best expressed by assisting his spiritual progress, not binding up the wounds on his travel frayed feet.

SUMMARY

Schatzgeyer contributed to the difficult and painful beginnings of the development of a Counter Reformation position. Beginning with a strong concern to engage the Reformers' positions directly, he came to rehearse and reiterate what he viewed as the traditional and correct statement of ecclesiastical institutions and teachings. The abandonment of a search for compromise enabled him to present a sharper and more coherent statement of his understanding of the Christian life.

The Reformers' rejection of his attempts at conciliation and his own hardened position made formal and permanent the division of Christian writers and Christian thought. By the end of his career one can indeed begin to speak of a distinct Counter Reformation theology.[54]

CONCLUSION

During the fifteenth century, the friars of Nuremberg were so confident of the future that they cheerfully dispensed contracts for anniversary masses which committed their services forever. So certain were they of their place in society that they inserted no contingency clauses. Within a century, their house was closed. Why did their fortunes change so swiftly?

The Observant reform was a failure in concept and only a partial success in practice. The reform did not raise fundamental questions about the friars' mission to society and their place in the social structure of the city. At most, the Observants can be credited with seeking compromise solutions to financial problems. But along with this achievement, the Observants created new tensions and animosities which replaced the financial questions they sought to resolve. The haughtiness of Observant purity served the order no better than had Conventual laxity.

The fate of the friars bears eloquent witness to the radical tactics used by the Reformers in the cities. As the friars protested so often and so bitterly, the preponderance of legalities was on their side. The reforming party—insurgent preachers and allied political leaders—annulled the established processes of ecclesiastical discipline and thereby destroyed the rule of the church hierarchy. The setting of norms for preaching and teaching was taken away from the bishops and theologians. City councils conspired with disruptive, crowd-pleasing preachers to determine theological and liturgical questions. The friars saw the disputations as mere façades serving to legitimize the bastard growth of the new order.

But the friars helped to fuel the fires which eventually consumed them. The ever more ardent pursuit of letters within the order together with the education of the laity helped set the stage for the Reformation. A learned, questioning critical constituency within the order and within the city was essential to the favorable reception of the Reformers' message.

Likewise, the very success of the friars in integrating themselves into the economic and political life of their

---

[49] Brismann, *op. cit.*, 18, 18ᵛ. See also Luther, "De votis monasticis," *WA* 8: p. 625.
[50] Brismann, *op. cit.*, 10ᵛ.
[51] Eberlin, "Wider die falschscheynende gaystlichen. . .," p. 44.
[52] "Vita," 154 R, 158 Y.
[53] *Ibid.*, 167 X.

[54] Hubert Jedin has quite properly criticized the term Counter Reformation as the only description of Catholic life and thought in the sixteenth century. See his *Katholische Reformation oder Gegenreformation* (Lucerne, 1946).

Schatzgeyer's published writings might be said to exemplify three stages: the search for reconciliation, the Counter Reformation and the Catholic Reformation. However, even his last writings are so much a reaction to the Reformers, the term Counter Reformation is an appropriate description of his stance. Another generation, including the Council fathers at Trent, could speak from a less embattled position host cities made them all the more vulnerable when the Reformation erupted. The success of the friars contributed an equal share along with their failures to the spread of the Reformation.

The plight of the friars dramatized the full range of problems encountered by those who sought a reconciliation between the parties to the conflict. By the time of the Diet of Augsburg the achievement of a theological consensus could not, by itself, bring peace. Empty religious houses and decimated bishoprics bore witness to a whole series of personal and institutional wounds which doctrinal agreement alone could not heal.

The opportunities presented to the friars for defense and counterattack were limited indeed. Before they could act decisively they had to perceive that the events immediately after 1517 were not simply the repetition of earlier conflicts. They had to realize that Luther was not simply another contentious scholastic. They had to realize that dependence on discipline by a bishop or provincial was no longer tolerated. They had to deal with an educated and critical laity.

Their strength lay in the excesses of the Reformers. Uproar and innovation, destruction and violence drove alarmed princes, in particular, to rally around the papal standard. The court of the Bavarian princes replaced the imperial cities such as Strassburg and Nuremberg as the titular capital of the South German Province. There those who wished to continue celebrating the mass in traditional fashion began to prepare an apology for their faith.

The eventual outcome of the conflict was a rupture of Christendom sought by none. Indeed, many of good will had hoped to avoid just a division. But events outran intentions. Attacks generated counterattacks. An incisive Reformer's pamphlet was answered by an obdurate "Catholic" statement. Whole friaries, provinces, or cities were assigned to one side or the other. Friar and burgher alike learned that conformity, not reconciliation, was the order of the day. As Europe's institutions fell captive to these divisive forces, no individual—be he even king or pope—could control the strategy on either side. A South German friar had to become either a "Reformer" or "Counter Reformer."

Finally, the friars suffered together with all of European society from the destruction of cultural catholicity which resulted from the religious conflict. Though cherished in a few cities, the friars were forbidden in some cities and restricted in still others. Unversities joined one side or the other. Censorship of publication, limitation of theological debate, and restriction on travel plagued the friars as it did all European intellectuals. Having abandoned the crusades against enemies abroad, the heirs of a divided Christendom took up the crusade against each other.

BIBLIOGRAPHY

Aktensammlung zur Geschichte der Basler Reformation in den Jahren 1519 bis Anfang 1534, edited by Emil Dürr and Paul Roth, **1** (Basel, 1921).

Analecta Franciscana (10 v., Quaracchi, 1885–1926).

BAINTON, ROLAND H., editor. 1965. *Concerning Heretics . . . an anonymous work attributed to Sebastian Castellio* (2nd ed., New York).

BÖMER, HECKTOR, and GEORG PESSLER. 1525. *Grundt und Ursach aus der heiligen schrifft wie und warumb die eer wurdigen Herren baider Pfarkirchen . . .* (Nuremberg).

BRISMANN, JOHN. 1523. *Ad Gasparis Schatzgeyri minoritae plicas responsio per Iohannem Brismann pro Lutherano libello de missis et votis monasticis* (Wittenberg).

Bullarium Franciscanum, Nova Series 1, edited by U. Hüntemann (Florence-Quaracchi, 1929).

Die Amerbachkorrespondenz, edited by Alfred Hartmann (2 v., Basel, 1942–1943).

EBERLIN VON GÜNZBURG, JOHN. 1896–1902. *Sämtliche Schriften,* Flugschriften aus der Reformationszeit **11, 15, 18** (Halle).

Epistolae Obscurorum Virorum, edited by Francis Griffin Stokes (London, 1925).

ERASMUS, DESIDERIUS. 1969–. *Opera Omnia Desiderii Erasmi Roterdami* (Amsterdam).

—— 1906–1958. *Opus Epislolarum,* edited by P. S. and H. M. Allen (12 v., Oxford).

GLASSBERGER, NICHOLAS. 1887. *Chronica* ("Analecta Franciscana," **2**; Quaracchi).

HUEBER, FORTUNATUS. 1686. *Dreyfache Cronikh von denen Orden-Ständen des h. Vatters Francisci* (Munich).

LUTHER, MARTIN. 1883–. *D. Martin Luthers Werke* Weimar).

—— 1930–1948. *D. Martin Luthers Werke. Briefwechsel* (Weimar).

Mittelalterliche Bibliothekskataloge Deutschlands und der Schweiz **3**, 3, edited by Paul Ruf (Munich, 1939).

MÜLLER, BERADUS, and VICTOR TSCHAN. 1964. *Chronica de ortu et progressu Almae Provincae Argentinensis . . .,* edited by Meinrad Sehi, *AFA* **12**.

MURNER, THOMAS. 1918–1931. *Thomas Murners Deutsche Schriften,* edited by Franz Schultz (9 v., Leipzig-Berlin).

—— 1939. *Thomas Murner in Schweizer Glaubenskampf,* edited by Wolfgang Pfeiffer-Belli, Corpus Catholicorum **22** (Münster/W.).

OECOLAMPADIUS, JOHN. 1520. *Oecolampadii iudicium de doctore Martino Luthero* (Leipzig).

OSIANDER, ANDREAS. 1525. *Wider Caspar Schatzgeyer, Barfuser Münchs, unchristlich schreyben damit er dass die Messs eyn opffer sey, zu beweysen vermaint* (Nuremberg).

PAULI, JOHANNES. 1924. *Schimpf und Ernst,* edited by Johannes Bolte, Alte Erzähler **1** (Berlin).

PELLICAN, CONRAD. 1877. *Das Chronikon des Konrad Pellican,* edited by Riggenbach (Basel).

PIRCKHEIMER, WILLIBALD. 1940–1956. *Willibald Pirckheimers Briefwechsel,* edited by Emil Reicke (2 v., Munich).

Reformation Kaiser Sigismunds, edited by Heinrich Koller, MGHssm **4** (1964).

SCHATZGEYER, CASPAR. 1525. *Abwaschung des unflats so Andreas Osiander dem Gaspar Schatzger in sein antlitz gespiehen hat* (Landshut).

—— 1516. *Apologia Status fratrum ordinis minorum de observantia* (Basel).

—— 1526. *Ein gietliche und freuntliche anntwort* (Munich).

—— 1543. *Opera Omnia* (Ingolstadt).

—— 1922. *Scrutinium divinae scripturae pro conciliatione dissidentium dogmatum,* edited by Ulrich Schmidt, Corpus Catholicorum **5**, *(Münster/*W.).

—— 1525. *Vom fegfeur* (Munich).

—— 1527. *Wider Herr Hansen von Schwartzenbergs neulich aussgangen puechlin von der Kirchendiener und gaystlichen personen* (Munich).

TSCHAMSER, MALACHIAS. 1864. *Annales oder Jahrs-Geschicten der Barfüsseren oder Minderen Brudern (1724),* edited by Abbe François Joseph Merklen (Colmar).

Urkundenbuch der Stadt Basel **7**, edited by Johannes Haller (Basel, 1899).

WADDING, LUKE. 1931–. *Annales Minorum,* first published Lyon, 1625 but cited from the third edition (Quaracchi).

CITY AND FRIARY RECORDS

Bayerische Hauptstaatsarchiv Munich. KU München Franziskaner, II, 2; KU Amberg Franziskaner, 5; KU Landshut Franziskaner, III, 2.

Staatsarchiv Basel. Barfüsser Urkunden Nos. 119, 127, 129, 136, 190, 195, Schwaz 41.

Stadtarchiv Frankfurt, Barfüsser, 1–7, 10, 15.

Staatsarchiv Lucerne. 519/9231, 519/9233, 519/9234.

Staatsarchiv Nürnberg. D. Urk., No. 168; Franziskaner Kl. Nbg., No. 4; 7 farb. Alph., 1859 Urk., 2029 Urk., 3159 Urk.; S. I. Lade 103, No. 2; Ratsbuch 12.

SECONDARY SOURCES

AHRENS, HAN H. 1939. *Die religiösen, nationalen und sozialen Gedanken Johann Eberlin von Günzburgs* (Hamburg).

BAUERREISS, ROMUALD. 1950–1965. *Kirchengeschichte Bayerns* (6 v., Erzabtei St. Ottilien).

BELL, SUSAN GROAG. 1967. "Johan Eberlin von Günzberg's Wolfaria: The first Protestant Utopia." *Church History* **36**: pp. 122–139.

BENZ, ERNST. 1934. *Ecclesia Spiritualis: Kirchenidee und Geschichtstheologie der franziskanischen Reformation* (Stuttgart).

BRÄNDLY, WILLY. 1946. "Johannes Lüthard 'der Mönch von Luzern.'" *Zwingliana* **8**: pp. 305–341.

BROOKE, ROSALIND B. 1959. *Early Franciscan Government* (Cambridge).

BUCK, LAWRENCE P., and JONATHON W. ZOPHY, editors. 1972. *The Social History of the Reformation* (Columbus).

BURMEISTER, KARL HEINZ. 1963. *Sebastian Münster: Versuch eines biographischer Gesamtbildes,* Basler Beiträge zur Geschichtswissenschaft **93** (Basel).

CHRISMAN, MIRIAM USHER. 1967. *Strasbourg and the Reform* (New Haven).

CLARK, FRANCIS. 1960. *Eucharistic Sacrifice and the Reformation* (London).

COULTON, G. G. 1923–1950. *Five Centuries of Religion* (4 v., Cambridge).

DEGLER-SPENGLER, BRIGITTE. 1969, 1970. "Die Beginnen in Basel." *Basler Zeitschrift für Geschichte und Altertumskunde* **69**: pp. 5–83; **70**: pp. 29–118.

DEMUTH, MAURITIUS. 1917. "Johannes Winzler, ein Franziskaner aus der Reformationszeit." *FS* **4**: pp. 254–294.

DOELLE, FERDINAND. 1921. *Die Martinianische Reformbewegung in der Sächsischen Franziskanerprovinz (Mittel-und Nordost Deutschland) im 15 und 16 Jahrhundert,* Franziskanische Studien Beiheft **7** (Münster/W.).

EHRLE, FRANZ. 1887, 1888. "Die Spiritualen, ihr Verhältnis zum Franziskanerorden und zu den Fraticellen." *Archiv für Litteratur und Kirchengeschichte des Mittelalters* **3**: pp. 553–623; **4**: pp. 1–190.

ENGELHARDT, ADOLF. 1936. "Die Reformation in Nürnberg." *Mitteilungen des Vereins für Geschichte der Stadt Nürnberg* **33**.

ERLER, ADALBERT. 1956. *Thomas Murner als Jurist* (Frankfurt).

EUBEL, CONRAD. "Die Klöster der alten oberdeutschen Minoritenprovinz" (unpublished typescript held by the Friedsam Library of St. Bonaventure University; St. Bonaventure, N.Y.).

—— 1886. *Geschichte der oberdeutschen (Strassburger) Minoriten-Provinz* (Würzburg).

FRANK, BARBARA. 1973. *Das Erfurter Peterkloster im 15. Jahrhundert,* Studien zur Germania Sacra **11** (Göttingen).

GATZ, JOHANNES. 1958. "Ulm." *AFA* **2**: pp. 5–41.

GRÄN, SIGFRID. 1960. "Frankfurt/Main." *AFA* **6**: pp. 120–170.

HAGEN, KENNETH. 1972. "From Testament to Covenant in the Early Sixteenth Century." *Sixteenth Century Journal* **3**, 1: pp. 1–24.

HEER, FRIEDRICH. 1960. *Die Dritte Kraft: Der europäische Humanismus zwischen den Fronten des Konfessionellen Zeitalters* (Frankfurt/M.).

—— 1962. *The Medieval World,* translated by Janet Sondheimer (New York).

HERMELINK, HEINRICH. 1906. *Die Theologische Fakultät in Tübingen vor der Reformation* (Tübingen).

HOFER, JOHANNES. 1964. *Johannes Kapistran* (2nd. ed., 2 v., Heidelberg).

HOLZAPFEL, HERIBERT. 1909. *Handbuch der Geschichte des Franziskanerordens* (Freiburg/Br.).

HUBER, RAPHAEL M. 1944. *A Documented History of the Franciscan Order* (Milwaukee).

ISERLOH, ERWIN. 1952. *Der Kampf um die Messe in den ersten Jahren der Auseinandersetzung mit Luther,* Katholisches Leben und Kämpfen in Zeitalter der Glaubensspaltung **10** (Münster/W., 1952).

—— 1961. "Der Wert der Messe in der Diskussion der Theologen vom Mittelalter bis zum 16 Jahrhundert." *Zeitschrift für Katholische Theologie* **83**: pp. 44–79.

—— 1950. *Die Eucharistie in der Darstellung des Johannes Eck,* Reformationsgeschichtliche Studien und Texte **73/74** (Münster/W.).

JEDIN, HUBERT. 1946. *Katholische Reformation oder Gegenreformation* (Lucerne).

JUNG, ANDRÉ. 1830. *Beiträge zu der Geschichte der Reformation* (Strasbourg and Leipzig).

KAWERAU, WALDEMAR. 1890. *Thomas Murner und die Kirche des Mittelalters,* Schriften des Vereins für Reformationsgeschichte **30** (Halle).

KEEN, MAURICE. 1971. *The Pelican History of Medieval Europe* (Aylesbury).

KIESSLING, ROLF. 1971. *Bürgerliche Gesellschaft und Kirche in Augsburg in Spätmittelalter,* Abhandlungen zur Geschichte der Stadt Augsburg **19** (Augsburg).

KÖNNEKER, BARBARA. 1966. *Wesen und Wandlung der Narrenidee im Zeitalter des Humanismus. Brant, Murner, Erasmus* (Wiesbaden).

LANDMANN, FLORENTINUS. 1928. "Zum Predigtwesen der Strassburger Franziskanerprovinz in der letzten Zeit des Mittelalters." *FS* **15**: pp. 96–120, 316–348.

LE GOFF, JACQUES. 1970. "Ordres mendiants et urbanisation dans la France médiévale, État de l'enquête," *Annales* **25**: pp. 924–946.

LIEBENAU, THEODOR VON. 1913. *Der Franziskaner Dr. Thomas Murner,* Erläuterungen und Ergänzungen zu Janssens Geschichte des Deutschen Volkes **9** 4/5 (Freiburg/Br.).

LOHSE, BERNHARD. 1963. *Mönchtum und Reformation: Luther's Auseinandersetzung mit dem Mönchsideal des Mittelalters* (Göttingen).

LOPEZ, ROBERT S. 1967. *The Birth of Europe* (New York).

MAEDER, KURT. 1970. *Die Via Media in der Schweizerischen Reformation,* Zürcher Beiträge zur Reformationsgeschichte **2** (Zurich).

MINGES, PARTHENIUS. 1896. *Geschichte der Franziskaner in Bayern* (Munich).

MOORMAN, JOHN. 1968. *A History of the Franciscan Order From its Origins to the Year 1517* (Oxford).

NATALE, HERBERT. 1957. *Das Verhältnis des Klerus zur Stadtgemeinde im spätmittelalterlichen Frankfurt* (Frankfurt).

NYHUS, PAUL L. 1970. "Caspar Schatzgeyer and Conrad Pellican: The Triumph of Dissension in the Early Sixteenth Century." *Archiv für Reformationsgeschichte* **61**: pp. 179–204.

—— 1972. "The Observant Reform Movement in Southern Germany." *Franciscan Studies* **32**, Annual X: pp. 154–167.

OBERMAN, HEIKO AUGUSTINUS. 1963. *The Harvest of Medieval Theology* (Cambridge, Mass.).

OLIGER, LIVARIUS. 1916. "De Relatione inter Observantium Querimonias Constantienses (1415) et Ubertini Casalensis Quoddam Scriptum." *AFH* **9**: pp. 3–41.

PAULUS, NIKOLAUS. 1898. *Kaspar Schatzgeyer, Ein Vorkämpfer der katholischen Kirche gegen Luther in Süddeutschland,* Strassburger Theologische Studien **3**, 1 (Strasbourg).

PFEIFFER, GERHARD. 1952. "Die Einführung der Reformation in Nürnberg als kirchenrechtliches und bekenntniskundliches Problem." *Blätter für deutsche Landesgeschichte* **89**: pp. 112–133.

—— editor. 1971. *Nürnberg-Geschichte einer europäischen Stadt* (Munich).

PICKEL, G. 1912, 1913. "Geschichte des Barfusserklosters in Nürnberg." *Beiträge zur bayerischen Kirchengeschichte* **18**: pp. 244–265 and **19**: pp. 1–22.

PLANITZ, HANS. 1965. *Die Deutsche Stadt im Mittelalter* (2nd ed., Graz-Cologne).

RAPP, DR. 1961. "Strassburg." *AFA* **8**: pp. 5–30.

REICKE, EMIL. 1896. *Geschichte der Reichstadt Nürnberg* (Nuremberg).

RIGGENBACH, BERNHARD. 1894. "Die Barfüsserkirche als Geburtsstätte der Reformation." In: *Festbuch zur Eröffnung des historischen Museums* (Basel).

—— 1967. *John Eberlin von Günzburg und sein Reformprogramm* (2nd ed., Nieuwkoop).

ROGGEN, HERIBERT. 1964. "Die Lebensform des hl. Franziskus in ihrem Verhältnis zur Gesellschaft Italiens." *FS* **46**: pp. 2–57, 287–321.

ROTH, CECIL. 1959. *The Jews in the Renaissance* (Philadelphia).

ROTH, FRIEDRICH. 1901. *Augsburgs Reformationsgeschichte* (4 v., Munich).

ROTH, PAUL. 1942. *Durchbruch und Festsetzung der Reformation in Basel,* Basler Beiträge zur Geschichtswissenschaft **8** (Basel).

RUSSELL, JEFFREY BURTON. 1968. *A History of Medieval Christianity: Prophecy and Order* (New York).

SCHAUFELBERGER, W. 1970. "Zurich." *AFA* **15**: pp. 78–114.

SCHMIDT, ULRICH. 1913. *Das ehemalige Franziskaner-kloster in Nürnberg* (Nuremberg).

SCHMITZ, CAJETAN. 1915, 1916. "Der Anteil der süddeutschen Observantenvikarie an der Dürchführung der Reform." *FS* **2**: pp. 359–376; **3**: pp. 41–57, 354–364.

—— 1915. *Der Zustand der süddeutschen Franziskaner-Konventualen am Ausgang des Mittelalters* (Düsseldorf).

SCHOTTENLOHER, KARL. 1925. *Der Münchner Buchdrucker Hans Schobser, 1500–1530* (Munich).

Schuhmann, Georg. 1912. *Die Berner Jetzertragödie im Lichte der neueren Forschung und Kritik,* Erläuterungen und Ergänzungen zu Janssens Geschichte des deutschen Volkes **4**, 3 (Freiburg/Br.).

Schultze, Alfred. 1918. *Stadtgemeinde und Reformation,* Recht und Staat in Geschichte und Gegenwart 2 (Tübingen).

Seebass, Gottfried. 1967. *Das reformatorische Werk des Andreas Osiander* (Nuremberg).

—— 1967/1968. "Die Reformation in Nürnberg," *Mitteilungen des Vereins für Geschichte der Stadt Nürnberg* **55**: pp. 252–269.

Spitz, Lewis W. 1971. *The Renaissance and Reformation Movements* (Chicago).

Stahl, Amale. 1949. "Nürnberg vor der Reformation" (unpublished Ph.D. dissertation, Erlangen University).

Steinmetz, David Curtis. 1968. *Misericordia Dei, The Theology of Johannes von Staupitz in its Late Medieval Setting* (Leiden).

Stöckerl, Dagobert. 1917. "Das alte Franziskanerkloster in München in seinen Beziehungen zum bayrischen Fürstenhaus bis zum Reformjahr 1480." In: *Festgabe Alois Knöpfler* (Freiburg/Br.).

Straganz, Max. 1900. "Zur Geschichte der Minderbrüder im Gebiete des Oberrheins." *Zeitschrift des kirchengeschichtlichen Vereins für Geschichte, christliche Kunst, Altertums-und Litteraturkunde des Erzbistums Freiburg,* N.F., **1**: pp. 319–395.

Strauss, Gerald. 1966. *Nuremberg in the 16th Century* (New York).

—— 1959. "The Religious Policies of Dukes Wilhelm and Ludwig of Bavaria in the First Decade of the Protestant Era." *Church History* **28**: pp. 350–373.

Stüdeli, Bernhard E. J. 1969. *Minoritenniederlassungen und mittelalterliche Stadt* (Werl/W.).

Vauchez, André. 1970. "La pauvreté volontaire au Moyen Age." *Annales* **25**: pp. 1566–1573.

Wackernagel, Rudolf. 1907–1924. *Geschichte der Stadt Basel* (3 v., Basel).

—— 1894. "Geschichte des Barfüsserklosters zu Basel." In: *Festbuch zur Eröffnung des Historichen Museums* (Basel).

Winter, Vitus Anton. 1809. *Geschichte der Schicksale der evangelische Lehre in und durch Baiern* (Munich).

Workman, Herbert B. 1913. *The Evolution of the Monastic Ideal* (London).

Zoepfl, Friedrich. 1955–1969. *Geschichte des Bistums Augsburg und seiner Bischöfe* (2 v., Munich).

Zorn, Wolfgang. 1955. *Augsburg, Geschichte einer deutschen Stadt* (Munich).

INDEX

Agricola, Daniel, 19
Amerbach, John, 19
Augsburg, 6, 8, 22, 30, 31, 37

Bachman, John, 38
Bamberg, 17, 26
Basel, 6–11, 13, 14, 17, 19, 22, 23, 27–29, 32
Bavaria, 10, 13, 38, 39, 43
Bern, 6, 18, 31, 37
Bernardine of Siena, 15
Brant, Sebastian, 19, 21, 37
Brismann, John, 41, 42
Bucer, Martin, 30

Calixtus III, 13
Campeggio, 16, 30
Capito, Wolfgang, 30
Carlstadt, Andreas, 29, 33, 35, 36
Caroli, Nicolas, 13
Conrad of Leonberg, 19
Council of Basel, 9, 13
Council of Constance, 12, 15
Crusades, 9, 15, 43

Eberlin, John, 23, 31–37, 41
Eck, John, 19, 22, 23, 37, 38
Eck, Leonhard von, 38
Ellenbog, Nicholas, 19
Erasmus, Desiderius, 5, 29, 33
Erfurt, 15
Eugene IV, 13

Frankfurt, 6, 8, 13–15, 18, 21, 31
Fraticelli, 12
Frederick III, 13
Freiburg in Breisgau, 14, 16, 32

Geiler of Kaisersberg, 18, 21
Glassberger, Nicholas, 11–13, 15, 17, 18, 31
Grütsch, John, 17

Heidelberg, 6, 10–13, 17, 18
Heilbron, 17
Hemmerlin, Felix, 12
Hoffmann, George, 30

Hus, John, 25
Hussites, 9, 15

Ingolstadt, 13, 17, 23, 38
Innocent III, 11

Jews, 15, 16, 19, 21, 33, 34
John XXII, 12
John of Capistrano, 15, 16, 33

Keller, Michael, 31
Komberg, Peter, 31
Kraft, Frederick, 19

Landshut, 13, 28
Lewis, duke of Bavaria, 13, 15
Lewis of Bavaria, 7, 10
Linck, Wenceslas, 24
Louis of the Rhine, 12
Lucerne, 37
Lüthard, John, 23
Luther, Martin, 22, 23, 25–29, 32, 33, 35–43

Mainz, 8, 17
Mariology, 18, 20, 22, 41
Mathilda of Savoy, 12, 13
Maximilian, 20
Meder, John, 19
Meisterlin, Sigmund, 12
Melanchton, Philip, 35, 38
Mulich, Jeremias, 26
Munich, 6, 7, 10, 14, 38
Murner, Thomas, 18–22, 25, 30, 32, 36–38

Nicholas IV, 7
Nuremberg, 6–10, 12–17, 22–24, 26, 27, 40, 42, 43

Oberrehnheim, 37
Ockham, William of, 7
Oecolampadius, John, 28
Osiander, Andreas, 23, 26, 27, 39, 40

Paul II, 13
Paul of Trinci, 12
Pauli, John, 16–18, 21
Pellican, Conrad, 17–24, 28, 29, 33, 38
Petri, Adam, 29

Pforzheim, 14
Pirckheimer, Charitas, 19
Pirckheimer, Willibald, 10, 22
Puchelbach, Albert, 13

Radical Reformation, 36, 38
Reformatio Sigismundi, 11, 33
Regensberg, 6, 8
Reuchlin, John, 19, 21

St. Francis of Assisi, 5, 6, 11, 16, 29, 34
Schatzgeyer, Caspar, 16, 18, 24, 25, 27, 28, 33, 37–42
Schilling, John, 31
Schmitz, Cajetan, 11
Scriptoris, Paul, 18, 19
Seehofer, Arsacius, 38
Spengler, Lazarus, 22, 26
Speyer, 8
Spiritual Franciscans, 5, 7, 15
Staupitz, John, 24
Stöckl, Blasius, 27
Strassburg, 6–8, 10, 11, 16, 17, 19, 20, 30, 31, 43
Studium Generale, 7, 17

Trithemius, Abbot of Sponheim, 19
Tübingen, 6, 17–19, 32

Ubertino of Casale, 12
Ulm, 23, 31, 32, 35

Volprecht, Wolfgang, 26

Wadding, Luke, 15
Waler, Caspar, 16
Wiler, Franz, 19
Wimpfeling, Jacob, 20
Wintzler, John, 26–28, 31
Wittenberg, 23, 35, 38
Worms, 8
Wycliffe, John, 25

Zamometic, Andreas, 9
Zasius, Ulrich, 20
Zell, Matthäus, 30
Zurich, 6, 12, 18, 19, 29, 31
Zwingli, 19, 23, 29, 31

TRANSACTIONS

OF THE

AMERICAN PHILOSOPHICAL SOCIETY

HELD AT PHILADELPHIA
FOR PROMOTING USEFUL KNOWLEDGE

NEW SERIES—VOLUME 65
1975

THE AMERICAN PHILOSOPHICAL SOCIETY
INDEPENDENCE SQUARE
PHILADELPHIA

1975

CONTENTS OF VOLUME 65

PART 1. The Czechoslovak Heresy and Schism: The Emergence of a National Czechoslovak Church. LUDVIK NEMEC.

PART 2. Distractions of Peace During War: The Lloyd George Government's Reactions to Woodrow Wilson, December, 1916–November, 1918. STERLING J. KERNEK.

PART 3. Classification and Development of North American Indian Cultures: A Statistical Analysis of the Driver-Massey Sample. HAROLD E. DRIVER and JAMES L. COFFIN.

PART 4. The Flight of Birds: The Significant Dimensions, Their Departure from the Requirements for Dimensional Similarity, and the Effect on Flight Aerodynamics of that Departure. CRAWFORD H. GREENEWALT.

PART 5. A Guide to Francis Galton's *English Men of Science*. VICTOR L. HILTS.

PART 6. Justice in Medieval Russia: Muscovite Judgment Charters (*Pravye Gramoty*) of the Fifteenth and Sixteenth Centuries. ANN M. KLEIMOLA.

PART 7. The Sculpture of Taras. JOSEPH COLEMAN CARTER.

PART 8. The Franciscans in South Germany, 1400–1530: Reform and Revolution. PAUL L. NYHUS.

Q11
P6
n.s.
v.65
pt.8

JUN 17 1976